A Basket of Stones

Symbols of Faith and Hope

Gwyneth J. Whilsmith

Colonsay House
Hamilton, Canada

ISBN: 1-895639-06-9
© 1992 by Gwyneth J. Whilsmith

Colonsay House
Dundurn P.O. Box 33508
Hamilton, ON
L8P 4X4

Printed in Canada

TABLE OF CONTENTS

For Arthur

When your children ask in time to come, "What do these stones mean to you?" then you shall tell them . . . .

Joshua 4:6-7 (NRSV)

PREFACE

When writing anything autobiographical I'm always haunted by the question, "Who cares?" or "Why in the world would anyone want to read this?"

Several times, over the past few months, when friends asked what I was writing I squirmed uncomfortably, trying to avoid a straight answer for fear I'd be met with questioning stares of astonishment. After all, why should I think my experiences are any more worthy of putting down on paper than anyone else's?

The answer, of course, is that they are not. In fact, many people in my own acquaintanceship have led much more interesting, courageous and devout lives. But, unfortunately, most of them do not have the inclination or the time to set them down in print.

The reason I share some of my experiences is because I firmly believe that everyone's story has a universality about it — that my deepest place is your deepest place too. We all suffer black days of disappointment and sadness, but our hopes and joys also shine with a similar brightness. In telling our stories to each other, especially the ones that lead us closer to God, I believe we gain strength ourselves and give hope to one another.

THE LAKE

Chapter I

A walk by the lake is not for deep thinking. At least not for me. The steady whooshing of the waves, the bright sun glittering on the endless expanse of water, the wind pulling at my hair and whiffling in my ears drives every thought from my mind.

Our beach is fifty-two steps down a steep clay cliff. The view from the top is dazzling as Lake Huron stretches out farther than the eye can see, like a wide ocean or a deep sea. Sometimes it's peaceful, turquoise, and shimmering; other days it's ominous and black with huge white-capped waves crashing in on shore. Whatever its mood it overpowers me with its majesty and limitless breadth of energy which speaks of creation and eternity, both humbling me and elevating me.

Drenched in this view at the top of the cliff, I descend the steps, driven to compose some lofty hymn of praise to the Creator. But when I reach the bottom, and the cool water ripples and froths around my bare feet like old lace, the cerebration dissipates along with all the schedules and clutter left in the house back from the top of the steps. I relax, am emptied, washed clean, my mind and soul at rest.

But after I stroll on the edge of the water for half an hour, bending to gather up a few pretty stones, my memory begins to stir and I think about my childhood on a dried out farm in Saskatchewan in the 1930s where we rarely saw more water than could be held in a few mud puddles, and even they were rare. Those were the days when there was never enough rain to fill the cracks that split the dry earth, when our tender crops often withered and died in the scorching sun.

When an infrequent shower did fall, we children danced outside, skipping and jumping, lifting our faces to the rain, letting its delicious wetness soak through our thin clothes to cool our hot bodies. And if it rained long enough to leave some puddles, we dammed them up, trying in vain, to hoard them, connecting them with shallow trenches by dragging sticks through the mud that oozed between our bare toes in an unfamiliar but wonderful way. All too soon, the water dried up leaving only cracked hollows in the ground.

Now, all these years later, I live every day on this magnificent lake, and its spell is never broken. Several years ago, I talked to a woman who was born and raised within the sight of Lake Huron, but who later moved away. "I never got over missing 'that old lady' who was always there like a steadfast friend," she said.

I know what she meant. 'That old lady' gets in your blood and when you must leave her, you feel something intangible but very important is left behind. When you return, everything looks and feels so right again.

The lake may be a steadfast friend, but she is a friend of many moods and can never be taken for granted. Often she's gentle, sometimes unfathomable, and occasionally railing and belligerent. But as we would suffer the fussing and fuming of a much-loved ancient auntie, we also suffer the moods of the lake because of the blessings she bestows in her benevolent times.

In summer she pours forth many blessings when, under a golden sun, she glistens in a multitude of shades — turquoise, blue, purple — adding a cast of magenta when a cloud passes overhead. This tranquillity can come to a sudden end when a brisk west wind stirs up whitecaps as far out as the horizon and beyond, causing many a boater to scurry to shore for safety, and causing us to put off swimming for another time.

My husband Art is one of those hardy souls who waits impatiently for the first dip of the season. Some warm springs he takes to the water in early May, although the rest of us never believe him when he assures us "the water is just great!" For the whole of the spring, summer, and early fall, he swims every morning and late afternoon insisting the freedom and release from tension he experiences as he plunges through the waves cannot be described.

Unfortunately, I can't swim. I'm content to wade out to my neck and splash about like a beached whale. Even that is refreshing, and I know of no better way to bring down my body temperature on a torrid August day than to stand chin deep in the cool waters of Lake Huron.

In July and August, our beds are usually full of grown children, grandchildren, and friends. We eat meals at the stretched-out dining room table amid much bantering. We swim, build sand castles, and light bonfires under the moon with smoke curling up to meet the low-hung stars. Late talks go on into the night on the back porch as we watch the fireflies in the Russian olive trees — and swat mosquitoes. Waldo Emerson once remarked, "Do what we can, summer will have its flies. If we walk in the woods (or by the Lake), we must feed the mosquitoes." I like that. Nothing in this life is perfect; summer also means long lines of washing, stirring up pots and pots of food, and dropping into bed bone tired.

The almost perfect days of summer soon give way to the cooler ones of September and October. Rainy days change the lake to dark slate, and often, a mist hangs over it like a silken shroud. Life slows down; there is time for longer walks on the beach.

There are no seashells to gather as there are on ocean beaches, but there is always a wonderful array of beautiful stones lying in the sand. They change with every storm. From the first day we moved here I was never able to resist picking up some of them, lugging them up the steps to the back porch or piling them on the window sills until Art cried, "Enough. No more stones!"

It was too late; I was addicted and couldn't stop. Big stones, tiny stones, in all shapes and colours fascinate me and tell me stories. One basket holds my very special stones, many of which are reminders of God's many blessings.

RING OF LOVE

Chapter II

When our youngest son Braden was going through a particularly difficult time, I was deeply concerned for him and as I so often do, I walked down to the beach to stroll along the water. The wide lake, the expanse of sky, the gentle lapping of the waves against the hard sand soon eased my tension. As I prayed for God's guidance for Braden, I bent over and picked up a smooth white stone the shape of a large egg with two dark rings around it. They reminded me of God's all-encircling love.

Later, I presented the stone to Braden for a paper weight on his desk. "Whenever you look at this stone," I told him, "remember the top circle is the never-ending love of God that's always with you, and the bottom one is the love of your family that surrounds you too."

There are many stones on the beach with rings circling them. Some are smooth, others rough. There are dull coloured ones, while others are in beautiful shades of green, purple, or pearl white. One day I gave one to my friend Yvonne. It was pointed and sharp-edged, but it was a lovely rose colour, and what made it especially beautiful was a bright green ring around it. As I presented it to her I said, "This is to remind you that God always loves you."

Looking at this lop-sided, uneven stone, she remarked wryly, "You mean God loves me no matter what shape I'm in?" Yes!

When our daughter JoAnne was little we gave her a puppy, Tammy, for her birthday. The two were immediately insepara-

ble. Late one afternoon JoAnne grew tired and cross, but faithful
Tammy was still at her heels. When they got tangled up and she
tripped, she turned on him. "Oh, Tammy," she cried crossly,
"Isn't it bad enough I've got God with me all the time, without
you always following me!" Children understand that God sticks
to us, that He's always with us, maybe even when we wish He
weren't.

There's no more poignant story in the Bible illustrating
God's love and staying power than Jesus' parable of the prodi-
gal son. During the period our teenage son Robert was on drugs,
I read it over and over.

At first, I marvelled at the hands-off, permissive attitude
of the father. How could any loving parent not only allow his
son to travel to the temptations of the 'far country,' but even
give him the funds to go. It seemed ludicrous, and yet, I came
to realize this was the only way the son would finally 'come to
his senses' and make a change in his life.

It also amazed me that the father could forgive so readily
and place no demands on his forgiveness. When the son returns,
asking for forgiveness, the father brushes aside his apology and
immediately reinstates him to sonship, while he starts the plans
for a celebration. As Bruce Larson points out in his book *Setting
Men Free* (Zondervan, 1967) there are no recriminations, there
is no talk of dragging the son off to church, or of sitting around
sentimentally hugging him. The forgiveness of the father was
there waiting for the son before he asked for it.

The 'far country' our son travelled in was often not any
farther away than the main street of the town where we lived,
but it seemed just as remote and dangerous. Although we were
never certain of everything that went on in Robert's life, we did
have to deal with misdemeanours, skirmishes with the police,
and once, a headline in the local newspaper. He had always been
a quiet boy, but now he grew even more uncommunicative and
introspective. When he showed up for a meal or a shower, he
would sit, rarely speaking, at the kitchen table, his fingers
constantly drumming and his muscles twitching from the effects
of the drugs.

Robert was born two and a half years after our daughter
JoAnne. His was a difficult breech birth, and I was in labour for

many hours. The doctors told me later it had been touch and go for both the baby and me. We were both pretty battered, and in my concern for him we called in a well-known London pediatrician. "He's fine," he assured us. "No problems."

It was two weeks before we could leave the hospital, but even then, I wasn't out of the woods. Six days later, my uterus ruptured and I came as close to bleeding to death as I'll ever be. I can never forget how desolate I felt, as I was being taken out of the house on my way to the hospital, looking back at Art standing with a three-week-old baby in his arms and a little two-year-old girl clinging fearfully to his leg. I wondered how they would survive.

They managed very well, with the help of his mother and mine who lived near by. Art became an overnight expert in sterilizing bottles and making up formula, while my sister-in-law took over the washing.

In time, I was on my feet again, and Robert grew from a scrawny baby to a plump, beautiful little fellow with thick curly hair and big, wistful brown eyes. He developed normally, grew teeth, started to walk and talk, although he never became the little chatterbox his sister was. Sometimes we noticed he struggled with his words, becoming frustrated or angry if the other children laughed at him.

Kindergarten went fairly smoothly, but each year after that became progressively more difficult. By Grade one, his teacher was phoning to say he hadn't arrived, and when I went searching for him, I often found him hiding in someone's bushes.

He was dubbed a 'slow learner,' a terrible misnomer that places a heavy burden on small shoulders. He grew to hate school, and my heart ached for him as he watched his classmates pass on while he stayed behind.

The frustrating part for us was that he seemed so bright at home. Our family played many board games, and without fail, he was the one who first caught on to a new game, once the directions had been read to him. He loved Monopoly and would keep a game going for hours, days sometimes, with his favourite uncle, Irving.

At school, however, this quiet, loving boy was belligerent and unruly, seeming not to try to do his work. We had many

interviews with the principal and teachers, and although there
were two teachers who tried hard to bring out the best in Robert,
most of them just threw up their hands. He was a problem they
wished would go away.

The principal was entirely unsympathetic, blaming Art and
me for not being better parents. I always went away from our
meetings loaded with guilt. When Robert was ten, this principal
suggested Robert, Art, and I take some sessions with a psychologist, so for many weeks we drove the thirty miles to
London.

Very soon, both Art and I felt these trips were accomplish-
ing nothing. The psychologist became frustrated, and even
somewhat annoyed, because Robert wouldn't or couldn't open
up at his prodding.

One day, driving home, I was in deep depression. I knew
Robert dreaded these sessions, and I felt we were just adding
more weight to the load he already carried. He turned his serious
brown eyes upon me, "Mom, do we have to go back there?"
Almost without thinking I replied, "No! We're never going
back."

Then I prayed all the way home that I had made the right
decision. I told God I knew He understood Robert better than
anyone, and that from now on, I would put all my trust in Him.
It was one of the many times I felt His all-encircling love.

By the time Robert reached Grade eight, he was the biggest
boy in the class. I dreaded his entrance to high school because,
as imperfect as public school had been, I felt the high school
would be even less equipped to meet his needs.

Then I heard about a teacher, a former Anglican priest, who
had opened a private school for boys with learning problems. I
telephoned him to set up an appointment. After listening attentively as I poured out Robert's story, he said, "It sounds as if he
has a perceptual handicap." Perceptual handicap? I had never
heard the term before. "What's that?"

He explained a child can be born, not retarded, but with an
imperfection in the brain that, although it might be slight, could
hinder learning. He also said that a child's brain might be
damaged at birth or through an accident. Many children with

perceptual handicaps seem completely normal in every way except in their learning capabilities.

Arrangements were made for Robert to enter an institution for testing, and the results did show that there was slight brain damage, probably received at his difficult birth. What it boiled down to was that Robert, who had an average I.Q., had no difficulty assimilating what he was told or what he read, but he did have great trouble projecting that knowledge, both audibly and in writing.

The team of experts who conducted the testing assured us that with appropriate training Robert had the intelligence to go on to university and tackle any course he chose. It's difficult to describe our feelings as the pieces of the puzzle finally began to fall into place. It took awhile for it to sink in that *I was not to blame . . . that Art was not to blame . . .* that the reason for Robert's learning disability was beyond anyone's control.

The teacher who arranged for the testing felt Robert could be greatly helped in his private school where teaching was done on a one-to-one basis, and with special audio-visual equipment, which was a new technique at that time. The fee, however, was far beyond our means. Out of his concern and generosity, he offered us a bursary, waiving half the fee, if we could manage the balance. So, after eighteen years out of the workplace, I got a part-time job at the local newspaper to help defray the costs.

We sent Robert off to school, and I shall never be able to express my full gratitude for the one year he spent there. His reading and mathematics skills improved dramatically and he gained a self-confidence he hadn't shown before. Of course, he was homesick and couldn't wait for holidays.

At the end of the term he begged us to allow him to stay home and attend the local high school, promising he would work hard and keep up his grades. We were no longer eligible for the bursary, it going to another student, and there seemed no way to raise the extra money. Without much enthusiasm, we decided to let him try the local school.

It turned out badly. Accustomed to the one-on-one attention of the teachers at the private school, he was at sea in a normal classroom. We got reports of him skipping school, and we were soon back on the old treadmill. After his sixteenth birthday, he simply walked out of school one day and never went back. The road to drugs had already started.

He and his friends hung out at the pool hall, a place where no self-respecting parents wanted their children to be seen. In time, however, I looked on Russ, the owner, as a friend, not only to Robert, but to me as well. Often, when Robert disappeared for days at a time and our imaginations ran rampant, seeing him sick or even dead, I'd make a frantic phone call to Russ. "Have you seen Robert, lately?"

Relief flooded over me when he assured me that although Robert was looking 'pretty seedy,' he was still around. I learned later that Russ set strict rules about no alcohol or drugs on his premises, and that he had a genuine affection for these kids. The boys, and I guess there were some girls too, sensed his concern and shared a rapport with him they didn't have with their parents, and I know he turned more than one wayward young person around.

Years ago I read about a brave man who went into the worst parts of New York to show God's love to the gangs of kids who roamed there. Most had been deserted by their fathers, many by their mothers too, so they had no concept of a loving heavenly Father. He asked them to read and rewrite the Twenty Third Psalm, substituting the word shepherd with someone they felt really cared about them. One lad, after deep consideration, wrote, "The Lord is my car mechanic . . ." because the man who fixed his car was the only person he could recall who treated him with respect and kindness. I'm sure if Robert and his friends had been asked to rewrite the twenty-third Psalm, their transcription would have been, "The Lord is my pool hall operator. . . ."

In the middle of all this turmoil, two of Robert's best friends were killed — one in a high-speed police chase, and the other in an electrical accident. I wasn't able to attend both funerals, but what I heard of the one upset me greatly. The young man's friends were there, of course, and instead of hearing about a God who loved them, they got a searing sermon on fire, brimstone, and hell. What a missed opportunity for that minister, no matter how sincere he was.

It reminded me of what a Christian friend said to me one day, "What I fear, Gwyn, is that Robert might get killed in a car accident while he's still in all this sin and be damned to hell forever!" If I had thought for one moment that a loving God would send a foolish sixteen-year-old boy to hell for eternity, I would want nothing to do with Him. I knew the love I had for my son was unending, no matter what he did or where he went. Nothing, not even death, could change that. If my small, imperfect human love could not be extinguished, how much more enduring and forgiving was God's perfect, divine love.

Attending the funeral of the second boy, Bob, I sat at the back of the funeral parlour watching his friends, including Robert, file in. Most of them were skinny boys with long, lank hair, wearing tattered jeans and jackets, their young faces pale and taut with grief. Such a sad, motley group they were, and I wondered what in the world the minister would say to them — and to the bereft parents.

A burly, middle-aged man entered. His nose had been flattened by an accident in his youth, and he looked more like a retired prize fighter than a minister. Every eye was riveted on him. Sweeping his gaze over the mourners, his broad face filled with compassion as his eyes brimmed with tears. He began to recite:

Jesus loves me, this I know
For the Bible tells me so,
Little ones to Him belong
They are weak but He is strong.
Jesus loves me, He who died
Heaven's gate to open wide;
He will wash away my sin,
Let his little child come in.
YES, JESUS LOVES ME
The Bible tells me so.

Those young people had all heard that old children's hymn at Sunday School, or perhaps a mother or grandmother had hummed them to sleep with it. As they listened to those simple, healing words, the defiance drained from their faces, and the stiffness melted from their bodies.

Interestingly, when someone asked the great Karl Barth what all the thick books he wrote on theology came down to, he answered, "Jesus loves me, this I know." Deeply profound, but so simple it can touch even the most rebellious heart.

One of the worst days of my life occurred shortly before this when I was a reporter and women's editor of the weekly newspaper for our town. I had informed my editor I was tired of writing my column *Facts and Fancies*, which I'd been doing for some time. Although he was a stern man, he had a soft heart under his prickly exterior and was well aware of my Christian commitment. "Whilsmith", he said, "why don't you write a religious column?" I laughed, "Leave that to the ministers!" He kept insisting he wanted a religious column from a lay person's point of view. Finally, I agreed to give it a try.

What would we call it? We bandied around several titles, some of his hardly fit for publication. Suddenly, I said, "I know — I'll call it *Singing Waters*." "Singing Waters," he snorted, "What kind of a name is that?"

I stuck to my guns because, just a few weeks earlier, I had visited a retreat centre north of Orangeville called *Singing Waters*. I thought it a lovely name, beautifully apt for the place with its deep gorge and gurgling stream. Looking back, I'm not sure why I thought it a suitable title for a column, except that since singing waters denoted peace and contentment, I guess I hoped my column would give a lift to the newspaper, often the bearer of bad news.

Consequently, I began writing the column, trying, in a simple way, to express my Christian faith. *Singing Waters*, published for over five years, was picked up by three other weeklies, and attained a loyal readership.

Each member of the editorial staff was responsible for the layout of certain pages. I always did the layout for the Women's Pages and those containing the news from outlying areas. The sports editor did the sport and agricultural pages, while the editor was responsible for the front and editorial pages. In this way, it was quite possible for something to be printed in the paper without me seeing it until it came off the press.

On this particular day, I picked up the finished paper to scan it through. A headline on the front page jumped out at me

— Youth Charged With Shoplifting. I felt as if I had been kicked savagely in the stomach as I read Robert's name. In a daze, I turned the page over and there, staring at me was my own smiling face at the top of the *Singing Waters* column. The irony overwhelmed me.

Reeling with shock, I went to the editor's office and gave him my resignation. "Why?" he demanded, scowling over his bristly, red beard.

"Because you didn't warn me about that story on the front page, and because I just can't continue writing a religious column, giving the impression I have all the answers, when right now, I feel utterly defeated and devastated."

He fixed me with his piercing blue eyes. "Whilsmith," he growled, "you've done a lot of talking about this faith of yours. Now, how about letting us see you practising it!" His words stung. I turned and went home.

The house was empty. Going into the bathroom to splash cold water on my face, I looked in the mirror and was shocked at what I saw. My face was white and taut, with blue circles under my eyes. There were deep lines where I had never noticed them before, and although I was only in my mid-forties, I suddenly looked old. "What's happening to me?" I whispered.

As I leaned against the vanity, staring at my image, I heard the voice of my inner soul, "What's bothering you?" it asked, "the fact that Robert is ruining his life, or what people will say about *you*?"

In that terrible moment of self-discovery, I confessed it was having to face my friends and relatives. Shamed by that torturous revelation, I begged God to forgive me and take away my crippling pride. Of course Robert's life was the most important!

I came to another conclusion that day, however. As I looked at myself in the mirror, so worried and tired, I thought that as sad as it might be, if Robert's life ended in ruin, I could not allow my own life to be destroyed too. If I allowed myself to get sick, or became so depressed that I was of no use to myself or the rest of the family, nothing would be accomplished. I knew I had to unhook myself somehow from my beloved son.

I closed my eyes. Immediately, there sprang to my mind the picture of one of the hook and eye fasteners we used to have on screen doors. Mentally, I carefully picked up the hook (myself) and unhooked it from the eye (Robert). I would always love him and do all in my power to help him, but I was not going down the road to destruction with him. Immediately, I felt stronger.

I did go back to work and continued to write *Singing Waters* for several more years. I did not, however, change my mind about giving up my eldership in the Presbyterian church, where I was also superintendent of the Sunday School.

A year or two before, I had been ordained as an elder, the second woman so honoured in our congregation. The first was my good friend, Elizabeth Moore, but after she moved away, the minister, Reverend Wilfred Jarvis, called to say my name had led the list in the votes for a new elder. While I was honoured that the members thought I was worthy, I was very hesitant in accepting the invitation. I devoured the material about eldership that laid out all the responsibilities and duties. Unlike some other denominations, the Presbyterian Church ordains its elders for life. Only after a lot of soul searching did I make the decision to be ordained. I loved it — the session meetings, helping to plan the work of the church, and I felt very humble and privileged to serve the communion bread and wine.

As our problems with Robert increased, however, I began to feel ill at ease as an elder. I read and reread Paul's instructions to Titus for the appointment of elders — one of the criteria being that no one should hold the appointment whose children were unruly or had a bad reputation. Every time I read it, the words hit me like a blow between the eyes. After another long session with the minister, I finally convinced him I had to give up my eldership. Actually, because elders are ordained for life, I couldn't resign, I simply took an inactive role.

We knew Robert was running with the wrong people, but since he wouldn't let us or anyone else get close to him, there seemed nothing we could do but pray. And pray I certainly did — day and night. Not that I was on my knees continually, but every time Robert came into my thoughts, which was very often, I lifted him to God. I had the conviction that if I were faithful in my prayers, God would honour that faithfulness. Almost every night I woke to slip out of bed and into a little room we had at the back of the house to pray for Robert. I often spoke the words softly, but out loud, hoping they would not only reach heaven but would somehow go out on the airwaves to Robert's subconscious.

One day he informed us he and a pal wanted to drive out west in an old rattle-trap car. We gave him the money to go; I'm sure we thought it would be a welcome change for all of us. Braden was only ten, and we worried about how all the stress in the family would affect him.

Robert promised he'd phone once a week. The first call came in the middle of the night — the old car had broken down at Golden, British Columbia, and he and his friend were strapped for money. He told me we could wire him some at the Golden Police Station!

Art and I were so exasperated we were tempted to let him stay wherever he was and figure out the situation for himself. In the end, we decided to wire him some funds. Because it was so late at night, this could only be done in a city, so we phoned our son-in-law Stuart, got him out of bed, and asked him to go to the office and wire the money for us. "Why didn't you tell him to sell the damn car?" he stormed. But he finally acquiesced, pulled on his clothes, and went off to do the deed.

Robert phoned again from Winnipeg saying he was settling there for awhile. When two weeks went by without a phone call, we weren't terribly concerned but when three had passed with still no word, I began to worry. By the end of another week I was convinced something dreadful had befallen him. He had given me an address with no phone number, so finally, I telephoned a minister of one of the large churches in Winnipeg to see if he would track Robert down. He returned my call the next day to say he had found Robert living in a small room and that he seemed OK.

Of course, I was relieved, but I couldn't help feeling disappointed that the minister hadn't taken more interest in Robert, maybe asking someone in the congregation to take him under their wing. What a difference it might have made if someone had invited him out for supper or shown an interest in him, uncouth as he may have looked!

Months before I was deeply wounded when someone, not knowing I was within hearing, called Robert and his friends, 'the scum of the earth.' My heart almost opened up and bled, but it helped me realize how God felt when His own Son was crucified as 'scum,' and how He feels when we look at any of His creatures as being expendable.

In any event, it was a fifteen-year-old girl who picked up Robert, took him home, loved him, and got him off drugs. God does answer prayers in strange and wonderful ways!

Much later, we learned what Robert was doing during those weeks we didn't hear from him. Arriving in Winnipeg without any skills, he found getting a job much harder than he expected. However, just when his money was about to run out, he landed a job at a tannery, skinning the animals, which was probably a fair comparison to the job the Biblical prodigal son had of feeding the pigs!

He would not get his first pay until he had worked two weeks, so with the bit of money he had left, he bought three loaves of bread and a jar of peanut butter and lived on that until payday. He'd always been a picky eater, but the next time he came home, he wolfed down everything that was put in front of him!

Eventually, he found a better job, and in the next few years he had some highs in his life but many problems, as well. He and the girl who rescued him from drugs married and had two lovely children, but they were too young and had too much against them, including serious financial problems. Sadly, the marriage failed.

One of the most desolate times of my life occurred in a church in the strange city where they lived. I travelled there because after the marriage disintegrated Robert's distressed phone calls in the middle of the night made us very fearful for him. In their bitter anguish, he and his wife separated the two children, she taking the two-year-old and he the six-year-old. My heart ached because I knew these two little girls shouldn't be raised apart, even though I also understood why Robert felt if he gave up both children there would be nothing in his life worth living for.

His small business had also gone bankrupt, and he was almost penniless. To top everything off, when I arrived at the rundown apartment into which he had moved, I was greeted with the shocking news that a Children's Aid worker had accused him of molesting his little girl and had marched the bewildered child off to a strange doctor. The latter's thorough examination proved the outrageous accusation utterly false, but this ugly episode almost destroyed my son's self esteem, which was already at a very low ebb, and it shattered me. Later, when I visited the Children's Aid office for some kind of explanation, I was greeted very cooly. Perhaps they were worried that we might file a complaint.

More fuel was added to this already devastating situation when Robert picked up a young drug addict and tried to rehabilitate her. We humans believe if we can help someone who is in even worse straits than we are, it will somehow prove we aren't so badly off ourselves and improve our own sense of self worth. Very often this strategy does pull us out of our depression, but in this case, the pathetic girl was far beyond any kind of assistance Robert could render her. She was a pretty little thing, but years of drug abuse had caused so much brain damage that she was given to violent fits of rage. Actually, I soon feared for our lives and hid all the knives. After two completely sleepless nights, my little granddaughter and I moved to a motel. Shortly after, the poor girl went berserk, breaking every dish in the house and destroying everything in her path before she stormed out. When I thought it was safe, we moved back with Robert.

Although he went out every day to look for work, he was deeply depressed. Each night, he'd walk the streets for hours. When he failed to return by two or three o'clock, I became frantic, fearing the worst, and wondering if I should call the police.

Without a doubt, it was the lowest point in my life — pounds dropped off me in a matter of days, my nerves frayed, causing my hands to shake and my muscles to twitch. We needed help desperately and the church seemed the obvious place to look for it. Since I knew nothing about any of the churches, I chose the one closest, a large, well kept building about two blocks away.

Because it was the second Sunday in Advent, the auditorium was beautifully decorated with banks of red poinsettias and a towering, glimmering Christmas tree. The congregation rose as one huge wave when the organ peeled out the processional hymn which ushered in the red-robed choir, followed by two ministers, a woman and a man, dressed in their rich, clerical robes. Reaching the chancel, the younger of the two, removed his long, black cape with the graceful flourish of a gladiator awaiting his plaudits.

The Advent candles were lighted, the scriptures read, and I listened intently to the minister's sermon, hoping to see a glimmer of light or hear a whisper of hope. Her words, though familiar, held no comfort for me, and soon the torment of my soul took over again.

After the benediction, the choir filed out, their voices raised in praise which fell like a dirge on my ears, and the after-service visiting among the members only deepened my loneliness. Two people smiled and wished me good morning, but when I shook hands with the minister at the door, his eyes were already searching out those of the next person in line. I left, my heart heavy as a stone, feeling worse than when I walked in.

When human help is not forthcoming, one is driven back to depend on the only constant source — God, the rock of our foundation. Walking back to the apartment I prayed, begging God for His guidance, strength, and mercy. He showed that His eyes and ears are never closed.

The first answer to my prayers came when, later that day, Robert finally put his children's welfare ahead of his own and agreed to send the little girl back to live with her mother and sister. His wife, happy to consent to generous visiting privileges, made the decision easier.

Next morning, while we ate our breakfast, the phone in the hall rang with the news he'd landed a job! The company's only stipulation was that he shave off his beard. In less than two minutes he was in the bathroom, razor in hand. Ten years later, he is still with that firm, managing a clothing store. When he was young, there were days when we despaired of him ever being able to earn his own living.

In those days, children with perceptual handicaps or other learning disabilities were just shrugged off as the dummies of the classroom. While advancements have been made in the testing of such children, little has changed in educating them. I was distressed to read a recent article in the *Toronto Star* which claims these students are still falling through the cracks. Parents are sometimes forced to hire lawyers to fight for the right to have their learning disabled children educated, and even if they win the court battle, the number of schools with suitable programs is very low. Many private schools, including the one Robert attended, have closed due to insufficient funding. I'm sure the main reason for such lack of concern is that these children appear so normal. If they were deaf, or blind, or retarded funds would be readily available for their education.

Most learning disabled students, with proper education and training, become self-supporting, tax-paying citizens. Without an education they usually end up on the low end of the totem pole, on the streets, on welfare, or even in prison.

As Robert approaches his fortieth birthday, he is a mature, sensitive man with a new wife, and another lovely little daughter. Most of his leisure time is spent fishing, playing golf, and working to conserve the outdoor environment he loves.

Of course, God is never finished with any of us, but Robert's father and I are happy that our prodigal son has come as far as he has. We never cease to thank God for His faithfulness in keeping His hand on Robert all through those hard years. We know His ring of love constantly surrounds us and our loved ones, no matter, as my friend Yvonne quipped, what kind of shape we're in!

BONDED STONES

Chapter III

The rocks on the beach fascinate children. When our own were little, and we lived part of every summer at the family cottage, they spent hours gluing small stones together to form weird creatures and painting them in glorious colours. The summer Robert was eight, he found a longish, tapered stone with a flat bottom. With a few brushes of paint he turned it into a dapper man which still sits on a shelf — a little stone gentleman with bright blue eyes and a big red smile, sporting a paddy green suit with red buttons and wide blue neck tie.

Robert's girls, Jenny and Julie, who live with their mother in Portage La Prairie, visit us in the summer, and they, too, love to collect rocks. They like to glue smooth egg-shaped stones together to build a variety of birds and animals. One day, Julie brought me a flat rock on which she had bonded several smaller, round ones. On each she had drawn a face. "Look, Grandma, it's our family!"

This treasure sits near my typewriter, and when I look at it I see some happy faces, a few glum ones, some with yellow-marker hair, and others with brown. The one with the glasses and prim mouth I take for myself. It's a mosaic of an extended family.

If these little girls were to build a true mosaic, however, it would have to be of not one, but two families. The one includes their father, his brother and sisters and all their children, and Art and me, and the other one that they live with which is made up of their mother, their adoptive father and brother, two sets of

21

grandparents and numerous aunts, uncles, and cousins. They love us all, but I wonder if they're torn and confused sometimes.

The home I grew up in was as secure as the Canadian Shield. We may have been hard up during the Depression with no money for fancy clothes or other luxuries, but my brothers, sister and I were as sure of our family staying together as we were of the sun coming up every morning. It was a 'known' that families didn't break up. As children, we might suffer many disappointments, but we could count on the things that mattered most staying the same. It was the kind of stability that many of today's children never know.

Not that there weren't unstable families during my childhood. I remember one especially, with a drunkard for a father. A charming man when sober, he was mean to his wife and children when drunk, and because of his addiction they lived in a poor house, and had little food on the table. One day, when his wife was in the barn helping him with the chores because of his usual hangover, one of their little girls tried to stoke up the stove. Her nightgown caught on fire and she burned to death.

There were other instances of wives staying with unfaithful or cruel husbands only because they were trapped by the mores of a society that viewed divorce as the unforgivable sin, and where few women had the financial means to escape. One of my grandmothers was caught in such a marriage. She was my grandfather's second wife, his first having died in childbirth. Grandfather had his good points, but his violent temper and domineering ways often made Grandma's life miserable. When she died, he married again, but his third wife had more spunk, and when he started to rant and rave, she packed his bags, threw them and him out the door, and never let him in again!

There have always been unhappy marriages, but in past generations divorce was not easily accessible, and even if it were possible, ending a marriage was a horrendous step to consider. I'm sure many women, and men too, stayed in unfortunate marriages only to provide their children with a stable home.

Was that a useless sacrifice? Perhaps in some cases it was, where anger and abuse spilled over to burn everyone, scarring mate and children for life. In other cases, children were raised in homes which, although not as happy as some, were still safe and secure because their parents were committed to provide that for them.

This year I spoke with a young man who has been through a divorce and several affairs. He's bright, articulate, and charming. When I chided him on his generation's lack of commitment he answered, "Oh, we have commitment, all right, but to ourselves." Then, he quoted Shakespeare, "This above all, to thine own self be true. . . ."

I, too, am a firm believer in being true to oneself, but not if it means devastating another's life. To me, that's not being true to what is best in ourselves because such a self-centred attitude tramples under foot any sense of nobility of character. In my opinion, it is 'truer' to the human spirit to consider others before ourselves. Especially our children. They don't ask to be born, and those of us who 'beget' them owe them love, loyalty and security, as far as that is humanly possible.

I cannot, in any way, concur with women who breed themselves to a male just to experience motherhood in order to fill some inner need. The innocent baby is a pawn whose future feelings and needs are given little consideration. I know of one such case which is already a disaster even though the child is still very young. The Bible is right when it warns us that we reap what we sow, and if we sow in selfishness, the harvest may be very sad indeed.

Many of today's children live in single-parent families or move from family to family as their mother or father change partners. Many of our society's ills come from the breakup of the family, yet the 'normal' family — one made up of one mother, one father, and their children — is under constant attack.

If families are portrayed at all in modern literature and theatre, they are usually dysfunctional or dishonourable. And think about all the movies made in the past few years with single people raising babies. It's as if the movie industry is setting up the single-parent family as the norm, when it's a known fact that in the majority of cases it's still married couples who raise children. The forces of evil would like us to believe otherwise.

They also give the message that marriages that last are somehow bizarre, or even unnatural.

I'm convinced many of the marriages that I've seen end in divorce didn't have to. With just a little desire and commitment, and the concurrence to seek expert counselling, most could have been rescued. I read, once, that when a group of divorced people were polled, even though some had remarried, the majority felt their first marriage could have endured if both partners had worked at it with more conviction.

The trouble is many couples don't want that kind of struggle, and when the going gets rough, they just walk away, trying to forget it ever happened. I suppose it all comes down to priorities. If one feels a marriage is worth saving, either for oneself or their partner, or for the sake of the children, it's worth all the hard work and dedication. But if one wants freedom with no responsibilities or sacrifice, then, the cost of staying in a marriage is too high.

Marriage *is* hard work — the good ones just don't happen. Experts say a successful marriage requires 100 per cent effort from both partners. It's true that one person can't pull the whole load, but it is also a certainty that one of the partners often takes on more load than the other. Actually, over the years, I can only think of a few marriages where there was 100 per cent effort from both partners — some others have been very lopsided indeed. Sometimes, the unlikeliest marriages survive, while others that appeared planned in heaven, fail.

Most of us enter marriage for the first time knowing scarcely anything about what's expected of us. Our role models are often our parents, who may have some rather warped ideas themselves. These days, most churches offer pre-marriage counselling retreats, but it's my guess that very few couples attend, even Christian couples. For a step of such magnitude, many either enter marriage with blindfolds on, or with larger-than-life, fairy tale expectations.

We spend years learning how to practice our chosen profession, and a few weeks, at the most, ascertaining how to build a solid marriage. It might not be a bad idea if before anyone was issued a marriage license they had to produce a diploma proving they had graduated from a course on marital bliss.

There was no greener couple than Art and I when we said our wedding vows, and nobody more surprised when everything didn't come up roses. If we'd been living in this modern age, we'd have been divorced in the first eight months! Even though we'd gone together for two years and thought we were well acquainted, it turned out we didn't know each other at all. Both of us were the youngest of our families, somewhat spoiled, and used to getting our own way. Besides that, both were strong-willed, and after we'd been married a few months, it seemed we had nothing in common. I was gregarious, loved parties and people; Art was quiet, detested parties, and only enjoyed being with his own family members.

There were some rough periods, even some wilderness times when God bailed us out by answering our prayers for help. On our fortieth wedding anniversary I laughed aloud when the Bible verse for the day was, "I have been with you these forty years in the wilderness!" — proving God's staying power and His wonderful sense of humour.

We celebrated our forty-fifth anniversary this year, and one of the cards we received had a picture of a mismatched-looking couple on the front with these words, "Your marriage should last forever...it was made in heaven!" Inside it said, "They do good work there!" I slid the card over to Art, "What do you think?" He just grinned and handed it back.

I doubt if many marriages *are* made in heaven, mainly because so few people ask that they be. It's rare for young people to sincerely call on God for direction in finding the right mate. They are more apt to place an advertisement in the lonely hearts section of the newspaper or go to a singles bar in the hope of meeting someone.

Nevertheless, I do believe that 'good' work is done in heaven in helping to build a lasting marriage. For my part, I learned God truly is the source of the strength and wisdom it takes to get over the bad times in a lasting relationship.

The night before we were married, I had many doubts. For one thing, Art wasn't in the best of health, having returned from World War II with lung problems. For another, we had no money (twenty dollars between us) and I was the only one with a steady job. Besides that, housing was so scarce that the only place we found to live was one room in someone else's house. On top of that, my parents strongly objected to the alliance. Not much wonder I had doubts! But with the over-confidence of the young, I prayed, "God, this may not be the best of matches, but you know I'm a strong person and can overcome whatever difficulty comes along." Talk about arrogance — in less than a month, we were facing problems for which I was no match whatsoever!

Neither of us wanted to admit we'd made a mistake, so it may have been only pride that kept the marriage stuck together. Nevertheless, the holding on together through some very difficult times bound us more and more tightly and developed a loyalty and a dependence on each other that has never been broken. When the children came along, we both wanted very much to be good parents; thoughts of separating were unthinkable.

Well, maybe there were some days when leaving did cross our minds, but not divorce, and certainly not ever marrying anyone else. When we took our vows for "better or worse, in sickness and in health, till death us do part," both of us knew exactly what that meant! Today, it seems many couples don't feel that now is binding.

The years rolled on quickly, and we mellowed and changed and grew accustomed to each other's idiosyncrasies. More than that, we began to appreciate the other's meritorious characteristics and stopped harping on the shortcomings. Life is too short, and days are too precious to be in constant disagreement. Art learned to be more comfortable with people until, now, he quite enjoys a social evening out, although he told me the other day when we returned home from a party, "You know, Gwyneth, I can stand just so much 'fun!'" And these days, I'm probably even more content than he is to stay home on an evening and read a book or watch a good movie on television. It's a happy, easy relationship, and we're so comfortable with each other neither of us could ever imagine ourselves parted.

Every marriage is different, and what works for one may not be right for another. That's why each couple has to strive for their own nuptial salvation. I love the story of one elderly couple who had argued and bickered with each other from the very beginning. One day, the old lady said to her husband, "You know, John, it's not right for us to go on this way. I think it would be best if one of us passed away, and then, I'll go and live with my sister!"

We know two couples who are still together after more than forty years of misery. They live under the same roof, rarely speaking, filled with so much anger and resentment that it affects everyone's relationship with them. Surely it would have been wiser for them to separate years ago and build new lives for themselves outside those animosity-filled marriages. The one couple stays together because they don't want to embarrass their grown children; the other because they can't agree on the division of their assets. One can't help but wonder which is the greater sin — staying in a loveless marriage where lives are forever scarred, or closing it out to make a clean, fresh start for a better life. After all, although divorce is always sad, often destructive, and sometimes even unnecessary, it still is not the unforgivable sin.

Not every marriage should be saved for the sake of the children. Many times, it's better for them if they're taken out of a hopelessly abusive situation. I know one young woman who had the courage to pick up her small child and flee from a home filled with anger and violence. With a great deal of inner strength and help from friends, she raised her child to be a happy and well-adjusted adult. I also know several other ravished marriages from which the abused partner did not depart, so that the hurt and the unhealed wounds remain forever with the children.

Still, it's always painful to break up a marriage — to face the fact that all one's dreams and hopes are shattered. Both our sons are divorced, so I speak from experience when I say the depression, guilt, and agonizing doesn't fade for years, if ever. This anguish breaks over everyone close to them, their children, their parents, families, and friends. A friend who experienced both a death and a divorce in her family says dealing with the break-up of her child's family was more difficult than the death.

Art and I loved both our ex-daughters-in-law, and we sorrowed for their loss from our family. Even now, years later, my heart still aches. Maybe young couples wouldn't rush into marriage in the first place, or would work harder to save it, in the second place, if they knew how excruciatingly painful the break-up was going to be.

Most of our friends are still with their original partners, and recently, we've attended three fiftieth wedding anniversaries. It always makes me laugh when someone is interviewed on radio and asked how they've managed to stay married for fifteen or twenty years — as if they'd accomplished some magnificent feat! The problems don't stop at fifteen or even twenty-five years — some marriages still fall apart after thirty or forty years, for a variety of reasons. One partner may just get tired of trying so hard, yet unsuccessfully, to make it work, while the other may get bored and wander to greener pastures. When we ignore the fragility of our marriages, we do so at our peril.

Something else that intrigues interviewers is the recipe for nuptial longevity. I've often wondered how I'd answer that question, so now, I'm going to try.

What you do before you marry will have a good deal to do with the union's success or failure. First of all, don't leave God out of it, ask Him to help you choose a partner with whom you'll want to spend the rest of your life. God may not do this over-night, so be patient, don't make the mistake of becoming infatu-ated with the first person who comes along and smiles at you. Take your time; this is the most important step of your life.

On the other hand, there are those who are too particular, believing they've never met the right partner when, in fact, they may have met several. Their pursuit for perfection in a mate can easily leave them single for life. Because there are no perfect persons there are no perfect matches; that's why one has to be prepared to spend time and energy to build a good marriage.

It's wise to choose someone with the same religious beliefs as yourself. There are enough obstacles in marriage without quarrelling over the church the children will be baptized in. By the same token, it also helps if both the young man and woman are from similar backgrounds and raised with the same values.

Sometimes, education, or lack of it, can be the downfall of a marriage. If one partner has a bent for higher learning and wants to discuss philosophy and history, while the other reads only mystery stories and is just interested in talking about trivia, they'll find they won't have much in common once the rosy bloom is off their relationship.

It's unfortunate more couples don't discuss financial matters before the wedding because many marriages founder on disagreements over money. It will save you some grief if your intended has the same feelings as you have about spending, borrowing, and saving.

If you marry believing your partner's main role in life is to make you happy, you'll be very disappointed. While our spouses certainly do contribute greatly to our joy, the state of real happiness comes from within ourselves. I knew a young woman who was unhappy with her fiancé's shortcomings, constantly complaining he wasn't attentive or devoted enough. When he broke the engagement she was devastated, blaming him for all her misery.

Of course, there's pain when an engagement is broken. Rejection causes terrible hurt, but placing all one's faith in another person to keep us happy is a mistake. I've found one of the best ways to break out of sadness is to look beyond ourselves and bring cheer to someone else, because happiness *is* found in giving joy to others. When we're happy, people are attracted to us; when we're gloomy, they fly from us.

Marry someone with a sense of humour. Many a day was saved for Art and me by one of his laconic, witty remarks that forced me to grin, in spite of myself, even if I was angry!

Don't marry someone you can't talk to, and who can't talk to you. Lack of forthright communication causes marital disaster. As important as it is to speak your own piece, it's just as necessary to listen to what the other person is saying. There's pain in most relationships, and if you can't deal with it by exposing it and talking it out rationally together, the chances are the marriage won't be happy.

Never marry someone you don't love. There are those who marry for money, or power, or prestige, but a loveless marriage can be a very bitter thing. However, one needs to be sure that it's really true love that's felt toward someone else, and not just a passing infatuation.

Years ago, I broke an engagement with a young man whom my mother adored. Naturally, she was annoyed and scolded me for doing such a silly thing. "I just couldn't stand the thought of eating across the table from him for the next fifty years," I told her. "Fifty years!" she exclaimed, "Why, fifty years isn't half long enough for me to sit across from your dad." I gave her a wry shrug, and she got the point. If you can't think long term when considering marriage, it would probably be best to put the idea aside.

"To love and to cherish as long as we both shall live," used to be part of every wedding ceremony, and it's still used in many. But I've heard of couples who, composing their own marriage vows, promise to be true to each other "as long as we both shall love." If you go into marriage with the feeling you may fall out of love, in all probability you will.

My dictionary defines love as an intense affection or passion for someone. Cherish is defined as holding someone dear in one's heart. To be loved for one's beauty or sexual attributes may be all right, but passionate love can soon burn out. On the other hand, to be cherished is the most wonderful gift in the world for it means you are precious beyond value to someone else.

Once married, be prepared to make some changes — not in your partner, but in yourself. Any relationship changes us, but a marriage that's worth anything at all *will* alter you, perhaps in ways you didn't expect. Compromise is the 'big' word, with lots of give and take on both sides. You may win the battle by taking an uncompromising stand, but the paradox is if you win too many of those battles, you'll lose the war!

One person is never entirely to blame in a broken marriage, but most of us don't want to believe we're half the problem. Sometimes we think if we could just change partners we'd be able to have a good relationship; we have to remember we'd be taking half the problem of our last marriage into our next.

I used to have a great deal of trouble with Paul's admonition for wives to submit to their husbands — and even now, I still think he didn't mean husbands are always right! From what I glean from Paul in all his letters, he couldn't possibly suggest, for example, that a woman submit to a brutal husband who beats her and their children. He couldn't mean that because in the same breath that he uses to admonish wives to submit to their husbands, he exhorts husbands to love their wives as Christ loves the church. The word cherish comes into play again, because I believe that's how Christ loves the church — He "cherishes" it — holds it dear to His heart. If husbands and wives cherish each other, neither needs to fear being stamped on, or losing his/her identity. Self-sacrificing love is not being a doormat to anyone; it means giving oneself to another person, while receiving the same kind, sacrificial love from the other. Each partner must strive for both to retain their selfhood (their true inner selves), because when one loses one's selfhood, there is little to give to the marriage.

I feel sorry for young people today, who are searching for the right partner. Although the rise of feminism was not only necessary and too long delayed, it has built barriers between men and women. Of course, it's only right and sensible that women be equal in the opportunities and rewards of education and business, but the transition is making some men not only unsure of themselves, but also of what women expect from them.

My mother was thirty-six before she was allowed to vote. Although that seems absolutely absurd now, many men felt threatened by this move to emancipation. In time, those feelings gave way to the reality that women were persons in their own right. Perhaps in another generation, everyone will look back to these days when many men, and women, too, are still unsure about what 'equality' means, and wonder what the fuss was all about.

Perhaps because the roles of male and female were more clearly defined, couples of my parents' era, at the beginning of this century, were more romantic. A young man took seriously the wooing of the woman of his dreams whom he hoped to win as a partner — and he didn't rush it. My parents always reminisced happily about the wondrous five years of their courtship.

When I was young, we were engaged in the horrific war of the 1940s, when our young men poured overseas by the thousands, some of them never to return. But the songs we sang and danced to were full of romance, love, and hope.

We were the first women to be hired for jobs that had hitherto gone to men. Not only did we work long hours in munitions plants, but we took on many other so-called male positions. I was hired to manage a small office in Toronto that had been under the jurisdiction of a man before the war, and which returned to his control after it. I don't recall feeling any indignation or bitterness that I had to step aside for him, but I do remember being proud that I'd done just as good a job as he had!

The tide had turned, and things would never be the same. Women *knew* they were equal to men . . . although it took several years for the rest of the world to catch on! Surely if both sexes can agree we are equal but, oh so wonderfully different, we can get back to courtship and romance, and maybe even lasting marriages. There is nothing in this world that compares to the sweetness and satisfaction of a happy relationship between a man and woman. That's what God made us for, and it's worth working hard to achieve it. As I look again at Julie's little stone family, my heart opens up to that hope, praying that God will bless her and her sisters and cousins with happy and lasting marriages.

EACH ONE UNIQUE

Chapter IV

The members of Julie's stone family come in all shapes and sizes, each with a different face. Some have plump, happy faces, one or two are square and pensive, another, whose head comes to a point, is studious, while one is downright glum. Her childish art work captures the wonderful uniqueness found in members of every family.

There are, however, strong family characteristics that break forth in every generation. When attending family reunions I'm often startled to see the back of my son's head on a distant cousin, or my mother's merry, brown eyes peeking out of the small face of one of her great-great nieces. Particular features — noses, chins, or hairlines — *will* prevail in spite of intermarrying.

Art has the lovely blue eyes of both his father and mother, yet our three children all came with brown eyes because, I'm told, the brown eye gene is stronger than the blue eye gene, and brown eyes go back in my family for generations on both sides. Thank goodness, the children inherited their father's thick, curly hair, however, and not the thin, straight stuff I've put up with all my life. Although these offspring carry some of our physical traits, they are still, each one, unique. It's not only their physical features that are distinctive, their psychological compositions and talents are just as diverse.

Before we had any children, Art and I thought babies were all pretty much alike, and that if you just followed certain rules and practices, raising children would be no great task. Such was our ignorance, we didn't know every baby comes equipped with its own iron will and strong character.

We were also critical of how others brought up their children, sure they weren't nearly strict enough, didn't teach proper manners, and were raising unruly ruffians. We were like the psychologist who said, "Before I was married I had five theories for bringing up children. Now, I have five children and no theories at all." We had yet to attain that wisdom.

Recently, a thirty-year-old mother of three, all under ten, sat at my table and sighed, "When I see 'young' couples starting their families, I often wonder if they know what they're getting into?" Of course they don't, no more than she knows what she's in for when her children reach their rebellious years. It's probably just as well; otherwise there might be a drastic drop in the population!

I'm not really serious, of course, because the joys of parenthood, and especially the satisfaction of seeing one's children finally metamorphose into responsible adults, far surpasses all the worry and sacrifice.

As a family increases so do the joys, but, often, so do the worries and sorrows. Love is like that. The more you love someone, the deeper can be your pain and disappointment, and the greater the loss if they should die. Parenthood offers no guarantees; sometimes a child raised in a loving, caring home turns out badly for whatever the reason, while another, coming from a cruel or disadvantaged situation, will rise above it and turn out well. And how many good parents have lost a child to disease or accident through no fault of their own?

Because the risks are great, it's understandable why some couples decide against having a family, but I would not have wanted to miss seeing our children turn into the adults they are — and best of all, become our good friends. When you're battling a rebellious sixteen-year-old, he or she will never believe they'll ever be your friend, but it's amazing the difference a few years makes. I think it was Mark Twain who said when he was sixteen he never knew a more ignorant man than his father, but by the time he reached twenty-one, he couldn't believe how much the old man had learned!

Although it's a worthy accomplishment to become friends with your children, you are, nevertheless, forever a parent. A good friend, who raised four children to adulthood, sometimes phones to say, "I had to put my 'mothering' dress back on today," and then goes on to explain that one of her children dropped by for a word of encouragement or love. Our daughter JoAnne, who holds a stressful job, tells of having a horrendous day at work when everything went wrong. Finally, she put her head down on her desk and cried to her secretary, "I want my mother!"

There were times when, as an adult, I too, needed my mother or father, and even after they grew old and feeble, they were still a source of strength and comfort — a loving bulwark between me and the world. When they died I felt very desolate out on the front line by myself. Suddenly, I was nobody's child.

Art and I were married six years before I became pregnant. We both worked, had a set way of life, coming and going whenever and wherever we pleased. There seemed no need to change a thing.

We'd been married in Toronto, but lived there only a short time before my father called from Exeter to ask if I could come back for a few months to take the place of his bookkeeper, who had suddenly resigned.

Originally, I moved to Exeter, Ontario with my parents in 1940, where my father purchased a feed and grain business after they moved from the farm in Saskatchewan. On finishing high school, I completed a business course in London before returning to Exeter to work in my father's office.

Art's parents emigrated from England just before the First World War, settled in Toronto, and raised their four children. They moved to Exeter in 1942 when Art's father was offered a job there for the duration of the War.

When Art was invalided home from the Merchant Navy in 1943, he came to Exeter, and never having lived there before, felt strange and somewhat lonely. The Whilsmiths lived just up the street from us, and mother constantly urged me to visit that "poor Whilsmith boy," but I was having such a good time with the airmen who were based near Exeter I never seemed to have the time to do that good deed.

One winter's evening, however, when walking my dog, I ran into this "poor Whilsmith boy" and we strolled along for several blocks. Reaching my back door, I asked him if he wanted to come in. He did, and didn't leave until after 4 a.m., worrying his poor mother who thought he had collapsed in a snowbank! His recuperation lasted two years, during which period he spent a good many late evenings in my parents' living room.

When his health returned, we both moved to Toronto to look for work. A few months later we eloped, not divulging this news to either set of parents for a week, and causing something of a furore.

Later, my job was returned to the young man who had left it to join the Army, and Art, always artistic, started a small enterprise making beautiful leather jewellery, with which I assisted him in our small living quarters. When my father called, there seemed to be no reason for us not to return to Exeter for a few months, and although we certainly planned to go back to Toronto, that day never arrived.

We had celebrated the end of World War II in Toronto the summer of 1945, but the Royal Canadian Air Force Base near Exeter was still operating at full tilt. Because the town overflowed with airmen's families, finding an apartment was impossible. For a few months we lived with Art's parents, but eventually were happy to find two rooms in the upstairs of one of Exeter's large, old homes.

Construction started on a new high school, and Art, who had rarely held a hammer in his hand before, applied as a carpenter's helper. He loved this work and progressed in carpentry so well he soon decided to build us our own house.

Post-wartime restrictions on lumber were in effect, and what was available was very expensive. A friend of my father's, Percy Tyreman, told us about an old house out in the country that had to be torn down. Art ended up buying this derelict building for a hundred and fifty dollars, and he and Percy dismantled it, board by board, pulling out all the nails, and stacking it on a truck. Excluding the roofing shingles and the asphalt siding, there was more than enough material to build our small house on a lot given to us by my parents. Needless to say, its cost was a far cry from the last house Art and I built forty years later.

Despite its small size, it was a palace to us with a fireplace in the living room, a modern kitchen, small dining room with corner cupboards to hold my fancy china, one bedroom, and a bath. Over the years, we moved to larger and more pretentious houses, but the thrill never came close to the one we experienced in owning that first, tiny house.

A week or two after we'd moved in, a lady called to view our small manor and liked what she saw so much she asked Art to build a house for her. This was his first building contract and the beginning of a career he loved. In the next forty years he constructed dozens of houses in Exeter.

Three years after we moved into the house, I awoke one morning with a sick stomach and a dizzy head. "Phone Dad and tell him I've got the flu and won't be in to work," I wailed to Art. When these symptoms didn't subside and, in fact, grew worse with every passing morning, I dragged myself off to the office of Dr. Fletcher, who was also our neighbour and friend. After a brief examination, he smiled, "You're going to have a baby, Gwyn."

If I was somewhat startled by this news, it was nothing compared to the shock it brought Art. I don't think it ever occurred to him he might, some day, become a father. It took time to grow accustomed to the idea of being parents, but when my morning sickness finally, and thankfully, departed, excitement took over from shock.

Not that we ever envisioned the baby making much change in our lives. Why should it? We pictured a kind of living, passive doll whom we could carry along with us wherever we went like a watermelon in a basket. We knew there would be diapers to wash, and probably formula to fix, and that I'd leave work for a few months, but we viewed this as no big hurdle. As it turned out, I didn't return to work for eighteen years.

About two years before I became pregnant, we purchased a beautiful, purebred Scotch collie, Lassie. She was the most gentle, loving dog in the world, and we fussed over her as we would a child, bathing and combing her soft fur, and taking her everywhere we went. Sometimes, Art travelled north to build cottages, leaving Lassie and me to ourselves. Her usual custom was to sleep on a mat beside our bed, but when Art was away she jumped up on the bed to stretch out beside me, missing him and needing to be near the other person she loved.

Maybe it was wrong to treat her like a human, to shower so much love and attention on her. In any event, a month before the baby was born, when we were out for a Sunday walk, Lassie, frightened by some boys playing ball on the sidewalk, darted out in front of a car to be killed before our eyes. Our hearts were broken. Art's mother, trying to console us said, "It's very sad, but you must be thankful the baby is still all right."

She was right, of course, because when our baby girl was born in a few weeks, we knew that while we had loved Lassie, it was nothing to what swelled up in our hearts at the sight of the beautiful child we had produced.

JoAnne Marie, a pink and white miracle, was born in a London hospital. Neither her father nor I could have imagined anything so beautiful. Parental love swept over us in giant waves. Gone were any thoughts of carting her around like a watermelon; she would need the most careful and expert attention, and who would give it to her? Certainly not us — we knew nothing about babies. When the day came to take her home from the hospital, we went in fear and trembling. I wondered, as I looked down at her in my arms, if she would sleep so peacefully if she knew what a pair of scaredy-cats she had for parents. We banked on both our mothers who lived nearby.

Having no idea how to care for a baby himself, Art had very little faith in my expertise either, and constantly questioned all my decisions. It was fortunate that our mothers did come to the rescue, not only to help in the first few days, but to keep assuring us we were not complete failures. I also relied heavily on Dr. Fletcher who, bless his heart, came to my every call, playing down my fears and bolstering my endeavours at motherhood.

And if ever a baby was raised by the book it was JoAnne; Dr. Benjamin Spock's thick missive was always at hand. By the end of the baby's first year, it was tattered and worn, and I'm sure I'd never have made it without it!

JoAnne wrapped Art around her little finger at his first glimpse of her, so it wasn't surprising that he took to fatherhood as a devoted slave takes to a fairy princess. Her wish was his command and nothing much has changed since then!

Our first little boy, Robert, was born two and a half years after JoAnne. As I've described in Chapter II, he got off to a difficult start, but at least Art and I were a little more experienced and more relaxed. One of my friends says God should make our first child a throw-away baby, one we can just practice on to hone our parental skills for the 'real' children who follow. In practice, no one would dream of casting out their first, precious baby, but it is true that the first little one is prey to all our mistakes and lack of confidence. By the time one has become somewhat competent as a parent, one's childbearing days are over. Still, it always amazes me how most children overcome their parents' mistakes and grow up to be healthy, well adjusted people.

Art and I both felt our 'gentleman's family' of one girl and one boy was just right. When Robert was two, we moved from our first tiny house, to a larger one Art also built for us. It had a small bedroom for each child, and a family room in which they could play. It seemed the perfect setup.

The children got on well together, rarely quarrelling. Being the older, JoAnne was the leader, not only in their play but in their pranks as well. Some nights when Art and I watched television, we'd hear a little rustle under the coffee table, and there they'd be, snuggled together, watching along with us, when we thought they'd been asleep for hours!

Robert was stricken when JoAnne left him for kindergarten. Standing on the laundry box, peering sadly through the window as she skipped off to school with the neighbour's children, and with his tears overflowing, he'd cry, "Wan goey gooy." (JoAnne's going to school.)

JoAnne was a great little preacher, always taking her Sunday School lessons to heart. One day, when she was six and he was two and a half, she commenced a little sermon at the dinner table about God always being with us. "God is everywhere," she informed us, gravely. "He's right beside mommy, and standing beside daddy," and then turning her eyes on Robert, sitting in his highchair across the table, she ended, "and He's standing right behind Robert." Her little brother, his eyes growing round,

cast a fearful glance over his shoulder. "Go 'way!" he commanded.

In fact, God was with us and blessing us, and after we'd
been in the new house a few months, I broached the subject to
Art that we might respond to His blessings by offering to take
in a homeless girl. Art, always a very private person, was not
too enthusiastic about having a stranger in his home, but eventually, he agreed to me contacting the Children's Aid Society.
A social worker was soon sent to interview us and begin the
procedure so that we could become foster parents. Clare
McGowan was the executive director at that time, a lovely,
warm-hearted lady with great empathy for needy children. She
became our lasting friend.

Not long after the investigation was completed, we were
informed that a teenage girl was coming to us, but because of a
last-minute development in the case, this didn't happen. When
a year passed without us being contacted again, we gave up the
idea of foster parenting, partly because JoAnne and Robert had
grown bigger and there just didn't seem enough room in the
house for another person. We went so far as to inform the
Children's Aid Society we had changed our minds.

Nevertheless, a few months later, the social worker was
back on our doorstep with the news of a thirteen-year-old girl
needing a home. Sickness in this girl's present foster home
necessitated moving her immediately. "I know you said you had
changed your minds, but I thought you might reconsider if you
understood the situation," said the social worker. She explained
the girl was pleasant and in no way troublesome. We replied
that not only did we not have the room, we also now believed
we didn't have the expertise to deal with a foster teenager.

The social worker continued to explain that she had
combed the county, trying to find a home, but to no avail. "You
were my last hope. If you don't take her, we have no option but
to send her to an institution."

"What kind of an institution?" I asked.

"Well, actually, it's for wayward girls."

"You said she was a good girl; why would you send her
there?"

She sighed, "It's our only choice."

Art's eyes met mine. "What can we do?" I implored.

He turned to the social worker. "We'll take her for two weeks to give you more time to look for a suitable home, but we can't have her move in permanently."

So it was arranged for Anita to come to us the next day. Since she would share JoAnne's room, sleeping on the top bunk, we emptied drawers and moved furniture to make space.

The following morning, a million butterflies fluttered in my stomach as I waited. Somehow, I pictured Anita as a tiny, delicate blond, but when I answered the social worker's knock, my eyes flew open when I beheld a husky girl, two inches taller than I, looking out from questioning blue eyes under a mop of thick blond hair.

"Oh my," I thought to myself, "What a *big* girl!"

Years later, I questioned Anita about what she thought when she first saw me. "I thought, 'Who's this shrimp?'" she laughed.

Anita came for two weeks and never left.

It wasn't easy for any of us. Anita, having been uprooted from her second foster home in a year, was distrustful and on her guard, and as any thirteen-year-old might, she bolstered her own sense of self-worth by criticizing us, especially me. Our home was constantly compared to her last foster home which, in her opinion, was much superior. Her last foster mother could bake better, clean better, sew better, and was, obviously much smarter than I, too.

And she didn't exactly endear herself to any of us when she complained that JoAnne, aged six, was "spoiled silly," and Robert, the "worst brat" she'd ever met. She bossed them around until I had to step in, even though I knew she was only looking for attention.

We ate our meals at a built-in table, sitting on either side. Anita ate with the enthusiasm of the always-hungry young, yet, she grumbled that we kept all the food at the other end of the table. Muttering away, while stuffing herself, she complained she *never* got enough to eat!

She had arrived with mismatched, handed-down clothes, and knowing how important it was for her to be dressed as well as the other students at her new school, I spent hours at the sewing machine turning out outfits for her. This was no mean task because I am not what you'd call a 'natural' sewer.

In those days, I could afford very few clothes myself, and it was an eventful day when Art handed me enough money to go to London and buy a new suit. Arriving home, I paraded around in front of the family, showing off my purchase. All were pleased except Anita. "There you go," she scoffed, "dressed up like a queen while *I* go around in rags." If I hadn't doubled over laughing, I think I might have killed her.

Her habit of chewing and cracking gum almost drove me crazy. One day, unable to stand it any longer, but not wanting to single her out for a lecture, I took both her and JoAnne aside to give them a talk on good manners. "There are certain behaviours that are not acceptable," I explained, "including chewing and cracking gum." Wanting to lighten up a bit, I added, "You know, girls, I'm going to make ladies out of you if it's the last thing I do." Anita, drawing herself up to her full height, and looking down on me as much as possible, sniffed, "I was a lady long before I met you!"

And what a lady! I alternated between loving her and wanting to wring her neck. In the long run, love won out, and over the next year there grew a bond so deep and lasting between Anita and me that it has never worn thin.

Knowing she missed her last foster family, I decided to take her to visit them a few months after she came to us. We were warmly welcomed, and I could understand Anita's affection for them. However, while she was out of the room, a friend who was visiting them turned to me and said, "You're wasting your time on that girl. You can't make a silk purse out of a sow's ear."

Crushed, I got up, called Anita, and left.

It's true she could still be obstinate and belligerent, but she complained less and less. And, as we'd been told in the beginning, she really was a 'good' girl, and most of the time she was bright and happy, with a humourous side that made us love her even more.

At the end of the first year, however, the social worker began to see that the bedroom Anita shared with JoAnne *was* too small. There were seven years difference in their ages and neither had space for any privacy. It wasn't fair to either girl, but at that time, we simply couldn't afford to build on another room.

The social worker's monthly visits became more and more stressful as she began to speak about moving Anita again. Clare McGowan, the sympathetic Children's Aid director, was brought into the discussions as the situation was considered from every angle.

The thought of Anita leaving us devastated me, and I couldn't even bear to think of what it would do to her. She had finally placed her trust in us and was feeling safe and happy. How could we pull the rug out from under this innocent, young girl once again? It was criminal!

I pleaded night and day with God to open a door, to provide the money to build on an extra room — to do something! Nothing happened; it was as if He had gone deaf. I tossed and turned every night, lost my appetite, and watched the pounds fall off. I simply refused to believe it was God's will to separate Anita from us.

The news got worse. Another foster family in the county could still not be found, which left only the institution that had been mentioned previously, as Anita's next home.

I reached rock bottom. One night, I raved at God, "If you intended Anita to end up in that institution, why did you bring her to us? Why are you allowing this to happen? What kind of a God are you, anyway?" I wept bitterly into my pillow.

At length, I grew quiet, and my thoughts began to wander over Anita's brief life. After the traumatic breakup of her own family, she had lived with a loving, elderly couple who tenderly cared for and comforted her. The Children's Aid Society, feeling this couple was too old to raise a young girl, moved her to the next foster home. In this home she learned many things, including sound Biblical teaching and Christian principles that would stay with her for life. In our home, her outlook had been broadened too, and again, she had learned new skills that would stand her in good stead. As I thought about all this, it seemed to me God's hand had been on her the whole time, always leading her along, step by step. The unwelcome thought came into my mind that maybe God was saying we had done all we could for this girl, and that His plans no longer included us. But it still seemed terribly wrong to send her to an institution for wayward girls, even if she would have her own room!

At last, I gave it up, and prayed the prayer of relinquishment, giving Anita's future over to God, praying that if it didn't include me, I would accept His divine purpose for her, even if it meant her going to that institution, which I still couldn't comprehend. As I left it all in His loving hands, I turned over and went to sleep.

The next morning I awoke with the great weight lifted, and even when Miss McGowan phoned to say she was coming to help me tell Anita she was leaving us, I still kept my composure. As we waited for Anita to come home from school, I told Miss McGowan about a recent trip to Alma College to visit a niece of mine. "Anita loved the place," I remarked, "and said she wished she could attend a school like that."

"Really?" asked Miss McGowan. A light seemed to come on. "Leave this to me," she called over her shoulder as she flew out the door.

The next day she was back, her blue eyes sparkling. "I've got a bursary for Anita at Alma College!"

It was too good to be true! Alma College at St. Thomas, Ontario, was a private school for daughters of wealthy parents, but each year it gave a few bursaries to girls who earned their fees by working in the dining room. Miss McGowan explained that all the privileges were theirs, that Anita would be at the college during school terms, but home with us for weekend passes and all holidays. It was the perfect solution — she'd still share the room with JoAnne when she was home, but her absence the rest of the year would give us all more breathing space. Only God could have worked out such a perfect plan, and I've never stopped being thankful that I finally stepped out of His way so He could engineer it!

Although Anita was impressed with Alma College when we visited my niece, it took a little persuasion to talk her into attending herself. Understandably, she didn't want to leave the good friends she'd made in the Exeter school, but finally, I convinced her that this was an opportunity not to be missed.

It wasn't always easy for the girls on bursaries. They had to rise early, attend to their dining room duties before and after school, and still keep up their marks. I'm pleased to say Anita did all these things well, commencing at Grade nine and graduating at Grade thirteen.

She was popular with the students and teachers, and during her second year was chosen a member of the May Queen's court, a singular honour. We watched her develop and blossom into a lovely and confident young woman, and Art and I almost burst with pride at her graduation ceremony as she walked in with her head held high, wearing a white dress she and I had made, and carrying a bouquet of red roses.

From her first day with us, Anita dreamed of becoming a registered nurse, so off she went to Hamilton General Hospital for three years of training. During her first summer holiday at home she met a young man, Rob. Because she was attractive and had a happy personality, there were always boyfriends around. So when Rob came calling that first time, we weren't especially interested, although I do recall thinking he was a very nice young man. That night, when she came flying into the house from their first date she exclaimed, "That's the man I'm going to marry!" "Does he know that yet?" I inquired. "No, but he soon will!"

Shortly after she returned to Hamilton she phoned, one evening, upset over what she perceived to be a problem with her birth family. After talking to her at some length, and trying to quell her fears, I turned from the phone and asked Art, "I wonder if we should adopt Anita?" He raised his eyebrows, "Would she want us to?"

By this time, we certainly considered Anita part of our family. She had been under our care for seven years, yet we hadn't discussed adoption mainly because she retained a tenuous link with some members of her birth family. That night, however, we decided we should give her the option. I phoned her back and asked, "Anita, would you like Art and me to adopt you?" After several seconds of silence, there came her smothered reply, "I thought you'd never ask!"

Although Anita was twenty by this time, we still contacted Miss McGowan at the Children's Aid to set the wheels in

motion. The case had to go before a judge who was somewhat
suspicious of a couple wanting to adopt a twenty-year-old girl,
so he delayed the adoption until Anita reached the legal age of
twenty-one when she could make her own decision. On the
morning of her twenty-first birthday, Anita, Art, and I were in
the judge's chambers where after a brief, but serious, consult-
ation, he signed the papers that made her a part of our family
legally. It was a glad day for all of us, one we've thanked God
for many times.

Two years later, after her graduation, she and Rob were
married in our Presbyterian Church, on a shining October day,
amid banks of golden chrysanthemums. What a beautiful bride
she was, and what a handsome couple they made as they ran
back down the aisle to greet the happy well-wishers on both
sides of the family.

While Anita was in her first year at Alma College, and
JoAnne was nine, and Robert, six, I awoke, once more, to those
familiar dizzy heads and sick stomachs; it was obvious another
baby was on the way. Rather hesitant to break this unexpected
news to Art, I was not only relieved but surprised by his
reaction. He was overjoyed! "Are you sure?" he demanded. "It
will be *wonderful* to have a baby in the house again!" You would
have thought it was the only thing he'd ever had on his mind.

Because of Robert's difficult birth, I was fearful of bearing
another child, but the specialist in London assured me, "This
time it will be different," and he kept a watchful eye on me all
through the pregnancy. He was right. In fact, I experienced so
little pain and discomfort at the baby's birth, I could hardly
believe the doctor when he exclaimed, "You've got another
baby boy!"

If ever a child was met with oceans of love it was our
Braden. The other children adored him, and perhaps because his
father and I knew this would be our last child, we looked on him
as very special indeed. There hadn't been a baby on either side
of our extended families since Robert was born, so attention and
love flowed to Braden from every corner.

JoAnne fussed over him like a little mother hen from the
first. The day we brought him home from the hospital I laid him
in the middle of the bed where he slept blissfully. A little later,

missing JoAnne, I tip-toed back to the bedroom and found her
changing his diaper as if she'd been doing it for all her nine
years!

Robert too, was passionately proud of his little brother,
stroking his soft little face and helping to feed him his bottle.
As much as he loved this new brother, however, he harboured
some secret fears. One evening when he crawled up on my lap
to snuggle close, he sighed, "I wish you were still my mommy!"
My heart tore, and I hugged him tight, explaining that no number
of new babies would ever stop me from being "his mommy."

Art and I always tried to be good parents; perhaps we tried
too hard, were too rigid in our discipline and our expectations.
Looking back, I feel sorry for JoAnne, because like so many
children who are the eldest in the family, we expected too much
from her. We wanted her to be mature beyond her years, setting
a good example for the boys, and looking out for their welfare,
as well. I believe I also hoped she'd live out some of my own
unfulfilled dreams. She took piano lessons, dancing lessons,
skating lessons, horseback lessons, to name only a few of the
activities we thrust her into.

Perhaps we placed too much pressure on Robert, as well.
Maybe we were too consumed with his problems at school, and
paid too much attention to those who tried to lay so much guilt
on us. If I were raising him again, I would just enjoy the dear
little boy he was, letting him know he was loved uncondition-
ally.

Child psychologists were just coming into their own. I read
every book on child-rearing I could lay my hands on; some of
them helped, others made me feel very inadequate.

However, by the time Braden arrived, I do believe we had
learned something about parenting. Certainly, right from the
start, we were much more relaxed with him. While the other
babies were kept on a strict, three-hour feeding schedule,
Braden ate whenever he felt like it and as often as he pleased.
We never worried about spoiling him, and there was always
someone cooing over him or playing with him. Always happy
and content, he responded with wide grins, joyful gurgles, and
excited waves and kicks.

When he was six or seven months old, we harnessed him
into a jolly jumper which he took to like a clown to centre ring.
He was a wild thing, swinging and jumping so high and wide
we had to move the jumper to a more spacious area for fear he
would bang himself on the door or walls. Laughing gleefully,
he'd kick and swing for hours. It was, I guess, just a prelude to
later years, when he often brought my heart to a full stop as he
performed rolls and steep dives and other breathtaking aerobat-
ics in his plane over our house, or staged a daring parachute
jump onto our front lawn! Braden thrives on excitement and
living on the edge.

JoAnne and Robert often complained we were 'a lot easier'
on Braden than we'd been on them. In some respects, they were
right. Because they were several years older, they broke the
ground, cleared the way, were the pioneers in our unknown and
untravelled land of parenting. When Braden was small and put
a ball through a neighbour's window or threw stones at a passing
car, causing irate complainants to storm our doors, we were
already conditioned by Robert's former escapades that included
wringing the necks of a neighbour's chickens and taking deadly
aim at a passerby with a pea shooter. While we understood
Braden's misdemeanours had to be addressed and accounted
for, we had also learned that they were the kind of tricks one
might expect, and the neighbour's wrath would eventually settle
down.

When Braden reached his know-it-all years, we had already survived Robert's and JoAnne's rebellious times; we did
not remain unscathed, but at least we were a bit wiser and still
alive! Experience told us most kids finally 'come to themselves,' eventually maturing and turning out fine. So, in many
ways, Braden *was* supervised with a lighter hand.

Nothing, however, prepared us for the social revolution of
the 1960s and 70s, with which our older children became caught
up. When Art and I were growing up, we often disputed the
opinions of our parents, but we didn't openly rebel. Although
there was illicit drinking among some of our young friends, we
had no experience with drugs or their life-destroying effects.
We felt helpless and totally unprepared to deal with what our
children were experimenting with. We were mystified when

they and their contemporaries laughed at our values, and hurt when they stamped on our moral and religious beliefs. And we couldn't comprehend why they rejected everything we worked so hard to give them — a comfortable home, nice clothes and education to equip them for life.

They cried "Love" and "Peace", yet, we saw much in their lives that was unloving and unpeaceful. When they began to live openly with people of the opposite sex, we were stunned and shamed. Of course, there had been sex outside marriage since the beginning of time, but it had gone on behind closed doors; therefore it shocked us to find 'free sex' flaunted on every side. What we had always held sacred was now deemed either puritanical or phoney. Many parents were caught in a biting trap, not wanting to alienate their children by condemning them so harshly they would lose them, but also trying to hold the line and maintain their own values and beliefs.

Of course, we didn't always know best, made mistakes, and sometimes had to admit the children were right. That was the case with JoAnne and her choice of Stuart. They met at college, and the day she introduced him to us we could hardly believe our eyes! Six foot seven, two-hundred-and-fifty pounds, his head covered with a thick, reddish-blond, unruly, six-inch halo of hair, he looked like a giant golliwog. Certainly not the man we pictured for our beloved JoAnne. It wasn't just his appearance. He was brash, abrasive, and set himself up as an expert on every subject. Despite all our objections, JoAnne's mind would not be changed; when they went off to get married, our hearts ached.

But she was right! Underneath all that hair was an extremely fine mind, and inside that big body was a kind heart as soft as an eiderdown pillow. The years mellowed him, making him much less intransigent; we love him as a son, and our times spent with him, JoAnne, and their dear little adopted boy, Owen, are always special.

What shocked almost everyone, twenty years ago, is now taken as common practice. Perhaps, as some people assert, society is more honest and tolerant in this wide open age, but I am not, to say the least, comfortable with or approving of much that goes on, believing what I used to say to the children years ago, "Just because everybody's doing it, doesn't make it right!"

In any event, despite all our parental mistakes and woes, Art and I are thankful that each one of our four children is an adult of whom we are proud. I think the old Biblical proverb, "Train a child in the way he should go, and he will never depart from it," is as true today as it was when it was first written. No doubt about it, the first years of any child's life are tremendously important.

I used to tell my mother she really didn't understand how tough it was to be a parent because when her children were growing up, there was so little to distract them or lead them astray. I also know that today's parents raise children in times far more difficult than I did.

As I think about our own dear grandchildren, six of them, ranging in years from four to twenty-one, I know they are growing up in a far less innocent age. But, oh, how I hate to see these children lose their innocence before they should. They know far more than children a generation ago knew at their age, and that's not always good.

I've heard experts say there never was a time when life was so good for children — they are housed and clothed better, they have more legal protection, their education is superior, and their health is looked after as it has never been before. Yet, when Jesus said we don't live by bread alone, I'm sure he included the children. Of course, we must strive toward the day when all children's physical needs and protection are met, but if children are to grow up to be strong, self-confident adults, they must also receive large quantities of love and support. No child was ever spoiled because he or she received too much love. Lavishing love on children doesn't mean encouraging them to be conceited, disrespectful, or mean to others; it means giving them a sense of self-worth that will never leave them. People who appreciate their own value are the ones who are self-confident enough to reach out to help others, and who can sustain either failure or success.

I can't finish off this chapter on families without speaking more about adopted children. As with one's birth children, there are no guarantees. Some are a blessing beyond measure, while others may cause great disappointment and even sorrow. Yet, it always maddens me to hear someone say of a child who has gone wrong, "Oh, well, you know he's *adopted*," as if that was the sole reason for his misbehaviour. For every adopted child who causes grief to his parents, there are dozens who bring only joy and pride. A parent prays just as fervently for an adopted child as a birth child, with the same burning hopes for its well-being and maturity.

The love is the same, too. My sister and her husband brought home their adopted five-pound twins, ten days after they were born. They, and the whole extended family, welcomed and loved those little boys not one mite less than if they had been their birth children.

Less than twenty-four hours after his birth, JoAnne and Stuart were in the hospital bathing their Owen, holding and rocking him all day long. Not only because they wanted to be there, but because their doctor felt it important that the bonding process begin as soon as possible. As with my sister's boys, this little fellow is as much their child as if he was of their flesh and blood. They cannot believe otherwise.

Yet, despite the bonding and the deep love that flows between parents and their adopted children, as the child begins to mature, something in his or her soul may begin to ripple and stir in a strange discontent — perhaps not discontent so much, as a feeling that something is missing. The child, naturally, begins to wonder about its birth parents. Who are they? Where are they? Why did my mother give me up?

I know some adopted children to whom these questions seem irrelevant; they are more than content to know no other than their adopted parents who nursed them through infancy, helped them with their homework, and worried if they stayed out too late. Others, however, are almost driven to find out more about their personal history.

We read many stories about happy, healing reunions of children and birth mothers, the latter probably having suffered guilt for many years. However, what may be a happy experience for the birth parent, may be a very disconcerting one for the adoptive parents who have always looked on this child as solely theirs. Now, suddenly, a complete stranger looms onto the horizon with whom they must share this beloved child. They can't help feeling threatened and unsure.

When the adopted son of a friend of mine told her he was searching for his birth mother, she was shattered, feeling she was being rejected. I don't think she was at all; he just had this unquenchable need to know his birth mother. Unfortunately, it didn't turn out well. Although he did locate his birth mother, and although she did agree to meet with him once, she wanted to keep the past in the past, and have no more contact with him. He then went through a period of deep depression, feeling he was the rejected one, and it took a long time for the relationship with his adoptive mother to heal. This kind of opening-up and letting-go requires a great deal of understanding, compassion, and prayer on the part of everyone involved.

Of course, it takes all those components to let any child launch out and finally take control of his own life. No child should be squeezed into the mold his parents choose for him against his will at any stage of life, but saddest of all, is the child who is never allowed to build up enough self-confidence to make his own adult decisions.

Some can't get out of the nest quickly enough. When our children were little, their favourite book was about a duck called Slappy who just couldn't leave home fast enough to see what the big wide world was all about. He ran into many difficulties, and was glad to come back until he grew up, but I'm sure the day came, even for Slappy, to leave home for good.

Some children, like Slappy, are in a hurry to test the deep waters despite all the dangers. Others are more reluctant, enjoying the security of the nest with all its comfortable benefits. They may have to be encouraged, and even gently prodded, to make the final move.

Because each child is different, he or she must be handled uniquely, but not necessarily equally. A woman I used to work with always made so sure she treated her children 'equally' that she calculated right down to the last cent what she spent on them at Christmas. If she went five dollars over with one child's gift, she felt guilty until she made it up to the others.

In contrast, it was our experience that one of our children always seemed to require more money spent on him or her or more hours of attention at a certain point in time than the others. In six months, the situation might be completely changed, but we strove (not always successfully) to meet the unique needs of each child at a particular stage. Because children are all so different, it's impossible to treat them the same. That's what makes them all so special.

I believe raising our children brought me closer to God than anything else. For one thing, I always seemed to be down on my knees praying for their health, their souls, their safety and welfare, or pleading for wisdom in my dealings with them! (Of course, this still goes on, even though they're grown and now the grandchildren are included.) God heard and answered those prayers, though often not in the manner I asked for or expected. Sometimes He said, "Not yet — wait," or even "No," and as disappointing as His "No" answers were, experience taught me He was either working out a better solution, or testing our faith in Him. I learned He *is* faithful beyond measure, and the words of the old hymn, "Trust and obey, for there's no other way," helped me through many an anxious time. Half the success of being a good parent is completely trusting God with your children, the other half is being obedient to His will, yourself.

Although dreadfully painful, it was often through my children, that God sandpapered off my own rough edges. Because of His constant forgiveness, patience, and long-suffering with me, how could I be otherwise with my own children, or with anyone else, for that matter? Often He scoured off my pride by humbling me, for no one can point the finger of superiority at another parent when one's own child has openly strayed from the path?

I owe a great debt to my children because I think I became a more understanding person, and a more committed Christian because of them. My prayer is that I never caused them to stumble along their way to God.

Paradoxically, while we all love our children, we can never possess them, yet they remain the most valuable and unique gift we will ever receive.

LIVING STONES

Chapter V

Our beach is rich in fossils. It's impossible to walk more than a few yards without finding at least one or two. When we first moved here, I greedily gathered up each one, bringing it back to the house, but soon my basket was overflowing, so now I'm more selective. Several I passed on to friends; two that were particularly interesting, I presented to a Japanese guest who wrote the following Christmas to say they sat in an honoured place in his apartment in Tokyo.

Our grandchildren are fascinated with them too, loading up their suitcases when they leave from summer holidays, dragging them back home to take to school. It's not much wonder they enthral us, bits of living matter from ages past, frozen in time — and to me, speaking of Eternity.

We often make the trip to Kingston in eastern Ontario where our daughter JoAnne and her husband Stuart reside. Because we travel that route on Highway 401 so many times, we usually read a book on the way, which helps to pass the five or six hours it takes to get there.

One time I tossed in a book I'd picked up at a sale — *The Natural History of the Great Lakes.* I thought it would make interesting reading for those of us who live on one of those lakes. I was right.

As we sped along, with Art at the wheel, I read. We refreshed our limited knowledge of the ancient sea that covered the Great Lakes area four million years ago, leaving great deposits of salt and slate. Even older than these ancient sea beds

are the rocks of the Precambrian era, some over two billion
years old, the oldest rocks in North America, that produced the
massive rock shelf we call the Canadian Shield.

It's hard to get a grip on a billion, or even on a million
years; how can we measure the few short years we have here on
earth against them — it is, perhaps, like taking the first tiny step
in a walk across Canada? However, when we read about the ice
ages, the last of which took place about ten thousand years ago,
it seemed almost close enough for us to grasp.

One of the most interesting things about this natural history
book was its designation of geological landmarks along the 401.
It advised us to look for drumlins, small tear-shaped hills
formed in the ice age, just east of Cobourg. And sure enough,
there they were, slipping past us like schools of giant porpoises.
It didn't seem so hard to imagine a great glacier moulding and
pushing them into shape — under the careful guidance of God,
of course!

The sarcastic question posed to Job by one of his critics
flashed through my mind, "Wast thou made before the hills?"
Of course, we weren't, no more than Job. God created, and still
creates with little help from us.

The history book also gave us more exciting information.
It said that at the point where the 401 converges with Highway
15 at Kingston, we could observe where the hardened sediments
of the bottom of the old ocean lapped over the prehistoric rocks
of the Shield. We had never noticed this phenomenon, even
though we had travelled the route dozens of times, and could
hardly wait to see if it was true. Turning off the 401 on to
Highway 15, our eyes earnestly searched the rugged sides of the
deep cut out rock. Then Art shouted, "There it is!" — a huge
mass of pink Precambrian granite lying under layer upon layer
of shale rock that had once been the bottom of a sea, millions
and millions of years ago, and on which much of Ontario rests.
We were as thrilled as if we'd discovered America!

As we looked at that huge pink rock holding up twenty feet
of shale, I could almost hear the triumphant shout of the psalmist
of long ago, "God alone is *my rock* and my salvation, my
fortress; I shall not be shaken. On *God* rests my deliverance and
my honour; my mighty *rock*, my refuge is God."

It's a pity some modern translations of the psalms substitute 'defense' or 'protection' for 'rock.' The word Rock is so much more powerful and pictorial. For me, a glimpse of the unworn Precambrian rock on the 401 opened up something more about the power and age of God, the Rock of our strength, who is not just a million or a billion years old, but who is from everlasting to everlasting — from no beginning to no ending.

We humans are bound by time — our days and lives are ruled by it. Although our years sometimes seem too short, most of us wouldn't want to manage more than ninety, or one hundred at the most, for who would want to live a thousand years in this world? Still, we live in a kind of paradox not wanting to live too long, but not wishing to leave life behind either. A wonderful lady in a nursing home, who has had her ninety-ninth birthday, tells me many times she can't understand why she's living so long, and how she longs for life to end, but then she adds, "but just not today!" Even at ninety-nine, life has its moments of sweetness and expectation.

We forget that with God there is no time, and although we cannot begin to comprehend what is a million years, to Him it is probably no more than the passing of a pleasant afternoon.

I remember this when I pick up a fossil on the beach knowing I hold in my hand a piece of creation from the dim, distant past. Some fossils are beautiful, like skeletons of those delicate flowers we see waving softly in underwater documentary films or as pretty as the wings of a butterfly. Once, while sitting on the beach, I idly pushed back some sand and discovered a fossil in the form of a perfect tiny clam shell. Many rocks are embedded with ancient ferns or squiggly coils of coral, while through others flow hardened ribbons that may have been living flesh eons ago.

There's a big black rock out in the lake that the children play on. It contains thousands of these fossils, messages from the ages. On my desk is a conglomerate, the size of my palm, that makes a solid paper weight. It's comprised of many different kinds of fossils all cemented together so firmly it's impossible to break them apart.

This fossil conglomerate, or 'pudding stone,' reminds me of the writer of the First Letter of Peter who had a vision of the

Christian church being made up of 'living stones,' I suppose one could interpret that as being the many denominations making up the universal Christian church. Goodness knows, there are enough of them, each with their own particular point of view for which many would rather die than change.

I heard someone say there are more civil wars in the Kingdom of God than any other kingdom, and I wonder why and how we can be sure our way is the only way to God. Civil wars within the Christian Church weaken it just as surely as they tear apart nations.

Whether the Church stands firm and secure or whether it cracks and crumbles really depends on us 'living stones' who make up the different denominations. Are we tolerant of another's viewpoint, or are we intolerant and judgmental? Sadly, it's not uncommon for some Christians, whether they admit it or not, to emit such an air of superiority when it comes to the beliefs of other Christians that the latter feel either humiliated or angry. Even in my own small community there are still closed communions and congregations who will not, or cannot, participate in ecumenical services. Non-Christians must wonder at our pettiness.

Jesus reiterated many times that we should first of all love God and then love each other. Over the centuries, so many trappings and rules have been added to Jesus' teachings that I sometimes wonder if He would recognize anything of Himself in our churches. Where the church should be the first place we look for love and human warmth, we often find distrust and icy rejection. One man tells me he finds more genuine fellowship in his service club than he ever finds in his church. Talk about slow learners — Christians must be the worst. Does God shake His head and wonder if we're worth all His trouble?

When the Church falls on hard times, and I believe this is already happening, Christians may be forced to bind themselves together with the beliefs they share rather than be split apart by their differing doctrines.

I was brought up in the United Church of Canada, my father being one of its most stalwart supporters when it was formed in 1927. I may have been 'submissive' but not very happy when I married Art and switched to the Presbyterian Church. Nevertheless, in a few years, I was more Presbyterian than its oldest living member, becoming very involved with our congregation. However, when I was in my mid-forties, I attended my first *Faith at Work* Conference which changed my Christian outlook forever.

The *Faith at Work* movement grew out of the belief that people from different denominations had much to learn and share with each other. Its premise was since God loves us all, we, in turn, should certainly love each other, and our faith in God should be put to work in every area of our lives.

This sounds a simple enough concept, but it was new to me. Never had I experienced such love and acceptance, such openness and such a willingness to share God's love as I did at my first *Faith at Work* conference. Sure that I had, miraculously, latched onto a wonderful secret that absolutely no one else in my congregation knew, I rushed home to convert them all!

Now these folk loved me, and being kind and long suffering, they politely heard me out, and then went back to being as they were before. I was with that congregation many years, and I never convinced one of them to attend a *Faith at Work* conference, even though I could hardly wait until the next one myself!

Of course, I'm sure the main reason was one I've already mentioned — they sensed my attitude had become superior and even judgmental. However, it didn't take long for God to bring it to my attention that while I was home reading my Bible, other members were out in the community giving food to the hungry, and drink to the thirsty, welcoming strangers, and visiting the sick. I breathed a prayer for forgiveness and rejoined my dear Presbyterian friends.

Nevertheless, Bible study became very important to me, and was heightened when my sister Lola took me on a trip to Israel. Many of our tourist guides used the Bible as a guide book, pulling it out of their hip pockets to look up references. I found myself breaking out in goose bumps as I viewed scenes familiar to Jesus, or stood on ancient sites mentioned in the Old Testament. Returning home, I was determined to learn more about both the Old and New Testaments, and it was then I asked a few church friends to join me in the study of Job one night each week over the winter.

At the same time I joined a small group consisting mainly of older Pentecostal women, two of whom were a sheer joy to be with. Their faces glowed with an inner light as they talked about being 'born again,' or recounted the day, or even the hour they were 'saved.' I longed for their assurance and peace. For weeks I agonized, wanting so much to experience their experience, to 'know' I was 'right' with God.

It was my practice to have an hour of devotions after Art and the children left in the morning. One day, as I sat on the chesterfield, I pleaded with God, "Dear Lord, how can I be sure I'm saved? *Am I saved?*" As I lay my head back, with my eyes closed, words, tinged with gentle amusement, flowed through my mind, "That was done two thousand years ago!" In some deep and mysterious way I knew it was true, I *had* been saved almost two thousand years ago on the cross. The only thing required of me was to believe it.

In passing, I must tell you I had heard those words, "That was done two thousand years ago," before. John Boyne, my young minister, at that time, had told me about an elderly repairman coming to fix his stove. As the old gentleman worked, the two conversed about religion until the repairman turned, with tears in his eyes, and asked, "Sir, have you been saved?" Sensing the old man's sincere concern, the minister laid his hand kindly on his shoulder and replied, "Oh yes, that was done two thousand years ago!"

When he recounted this story to me, I wondered secretly if it hadn't been a rather flippant answer to a serious question. But, that day in my own home, when those words rang through my mind, I knew they were true.

Many of my Pentecostal friends had what they called the Baptism of the Spirit, which meant they spoke in tongues. They often prayed in this manner, and although I didn't understand them, I did believe it was a spiritual gift to be sought after. I read everything on the subject I could find, had the laying on of hands and prayer, but I never received the gift of tongues. After studying Paul's first letter to the Corinthians, I came to the conclusion it was not in God's plan. Paul seems to be clear on the subject that no one receives all the gifts of the Spirit, and says whatever gift we receive from God, we are to use for the benefit of everyone. In his beautiful paean on love, in the thirteenth chapter, he stresses that no matter how great our gifts, they count for nothing if we are void of love, and stresses if we're going to strive for any gift, let it be for the love for our fellow humans. I never received the gift of glossolalia, although I know several people who do have it, including some Presbyterians!

Our small Bible study group broke up when the leader moved away, but I was determined to carry on. My sister had started me on a set of William Barclay's commentaries, which were more helpful than I can ever say. Taking the risk of inviting two friends to join me, I was surprised at their enthusiastic acceptance.

After a few weeks, one of them brought along another friend, Erni, a Roman Catholic, who had just lost her bright, popular eighteen-year-old son to cancer. This was really the first time I had been close to such an all-consuming sorrow, and I hardly knew how to react. It was pointless to fill the evening with trite words and senseless platitudes, so we just carried on with whatever book of the Bible we were studying at that time, and left Erni to listen quietly, hoping she would feel our love and concern.

When she left later that night, her face was so sad I feared we had only deepened her grief. I wondered if she'd return, but she did, week after week. Gradually, the hard shell of sorrow began to break until she was able to share the devastation of losing her beloved son and her deep insights about God. Soon, she was an integral part of that Bible study, all of us learning from her store of experience and wisdom.

One of her remarks I remember especially. At that time, Robert had dropped out of school and was on drugs. He would disappear for days, even weeks, and Art and I were often beside ourselves with worry, believing he would destroy his life. One night at Bible study I blurted out, "Sometimes I think it would be better if he were dead — at least I'd know where he was!" Erni looked at me with her sad brown eyes, "No, you don't, Gwyn. As long as your son is alive you have the hope he will change. My son is dead, and there is no hope of me ever seeing him again in this world."

Twenty-two years later, I know the utter folly of my statement, and the truth of hers. Our son did change, and his three children bring us much happiness. Erni's son's death stole that blessing from her.

That Bible study group grew in a manner no one could have foreseen. I never knew to whom I would open the door on a Tuesday night as more people arrived to join us. Soon there were over twenty sitting around in my family room, mostly young women, some of whom had business careers, while others stayed home to raise children. The rapport and trust that gradually developed over the years we met together was something none of us had experienced before, and perhaps, have never experienced since. It was beautiful — we truly were 'sisters.'

A more diverse group would be hard to find, some coming from prosperous circumstances, while others struggled to get by. There were women with deep beliefs, and others who grappled to find any faith at all. At least one had serious marital problems, and another, recently widowed by a car accident, was raising her three young children on her own. We represented six Protestant denominations and the Roman Catholic church.

Yet, we were one in the Spirit, as closely bound by our commitment to God and our love for each other as the fossils in my rock paper weight. Not that we agreed on everything, but each one was granted enough space to be herself. Once, after we'd attended a special service in one of the Protestant churches, Sylvia, a Catholic, observed, "It was great, but I missed the rituals we have in our church. It was kind of like eating chocolate cake without a nice thick icing!" Nevertheless, the healing and spiritual growth that went on in that group was tremendous.

However, Satan is wily, and he struck at our weakest point. Because there was such trust between these young women, they felt free to discuss anything going on in their lives, positive it would never leave the room. But the day came when one of them breached that trust by breaking a confidence shared within the group. The person whose confidence had been broken came to me in tears and anger. I was almost as shattered as she was, although I should have known this could happen. Erni was the only one I confided all this to, and we agreed the other young woman had to be faced with what she had done.

Now I am a great coward when it comes to confrontation, so how we prayed for the guidance of the Holy Spirit! I was afraid the guilty party would become defensive and stalk away from the group, breaking the circle.

At the conclusion of the next Bible study, I asked her to stay behind. Sitting beside her on the chesterfield, I took her hand in mine, and as gently as I could told her how she had wounded and disappointed her friend. I am amazed, even now, at her reaction. With genuine regret she admitted her mistake and promised to apologize and ask forgiveness from the wronged person. Then, she hugged me. "Gwyn, I know this has been difficult for you to do, but I thank you for it!" Two sets of eyes brimmed over.

After that, I was more careful about what the members shared with each other. I still think it's wise to confide your deepest longings and fears to only one or two people you know well and trust implicitly. Few of us ever intend to break a confidence, but given a particular circumstance with a particular person, it's easier to do than we care to admit.

Although I was 'designated leader,' my faith and understanding of God grew as never before while I met with those other women. They were generous in their tolerance of my beliefs but they forced me to look seriously at differing points of view. They asked for integrity, never allowing me to get away with a hackneyed statement of faith, probing with their sincere questions until my own doubts surfaced.

Now, years later, as I look at my fossil conglomerate, I gratefully remember all those 'living stones' who bonded with me as we strove to learn God's plan for our lives, discovering that He is the Rock of our strength and salvation — immovable, unchanging, everlasting.

SIGNS AND SILENCE

Chapter VI

The first of the many stones I picked up from our beach was the size and shape of a locket with a hole through it at one end. Years before, miles from here, I walked on another beach with a friend who suddenly bent over and picked up a small rock with a little hole clear through it. "Oh, good," she exclaimed, "finding a stone with a hole in it is a sign of good luck!"

Now I don't believe in charms, but that day, when I held the flat small stone in my hand and examined the hole that went clear through it, her words came back to me. I didn't need a good luck piece as much as I needed a sign, and I felt this was it.

Art and I had lived in Exeter for thirty-two years, making our living, and raising our four children there. It was, and still is, a good town, small, and friendly, and we felt very much a part of it. However, after the three older children were out on their own, and the fourth was about to leave the nest, we thought it was an appropriate time for us to make a change in our lives too.

We always loved Lake Huron, having shared a small cottage on its shores with family members, so we began to look for a lot on the lake to build a permanent home. Up and down we travelled searching for the perfect location, narrowing it down to two lots, one here at St. Joseph Shores, and the other further south in a much more populated area with more amenities. It was an important decision because we knew whichever we chose would be our home for many years to come.

Finally, on a hot summer's day in 1977, we had to make a choice and get on with our plans. We drove out to the lake to take a look at both lots one more time. The first was in a lovely area, wooded with big trees, and close to several friends. We had no trouble picturing our dream house on that lot. Then, we drove to St. Joseph to view the other location. It had only a few small trees growing on it, but it commanded a wonderful view of the lake which, on that particular day, was spectacularly beautiful with a fresh breeze rippling its multi-coloured surface.

While Art 'stepped' off the house to see how it would sit on the lot, I went for a walk on the beach. I felt foreign and uncomfortable. Only three large houses had been built in this new subdivision, all owned by strangers from the city. I worried that small-town folk like us might be misfits in this rather prestigious neighbourhood. Yet it was a beautiful location! As I walked along, I prayed for guidance in this important decision, and then my eye fell on the stone with the hole in it.

I rubbed the smooth oval rock in my palm remembering my friend's words, "A rock with a hole in it brings good luck." For some inexplicable reason I felt it was a sign from God that this St. Joseph's Shores lot was the place to build. When I rejoined Art, I didn't tell him about the stone because he really doesn't put much store in 'signs,' but interestingly, he had come to the same conclusion as I, and off we went to put our money down on the lot. (Later, we discovered we had wonderful neighbours!)

Not many people do believe in 'holy' signs, and some consider them laughable and bad theology. Those who do believe usually keep it to themselves, but every once in a while I meet someone who surprises me by speaking out.

One was my friend Betty who made her home in an institution for the elderly. Although she had experienced many difficulties in her life, she was always cheerful and upbeat. One day she confided that every morning she stepped outside the back entrance to pray, because she knew God was there. "How do you know that?" I queried. "Because after I pray He always touches my cheek with a breeze, and I *know* He's in that breeze!"

I believed her. For years, whenever I've felt particularly close to God in prayer, inevitably the words of an old hymn surge spontaneously into my mind. I find myself singing them without even being aware.

"Open my eyes that I may see glimpses of truth Thou hast for me; Place in my hand the wonderful key that will unclasp and set me free. Silently now I wait for Thee, ready my God Thy will to see; Open my eyes illumine me, Spirit Divine."

I don't know why it's the words of that old hymn God brings to my mind, except that I do know I constantly need glimpses of His truth, and I do desire to be set free from my fears and inhibitions. I know, also, although I cannot explain it, that He is blessing me in those words. I know it because, like Betty, I *know* it!

The first of God's signs I remember witnessing was when I was about eight. As I mentioned before, we lived on a dry Saskatchewan farm during the drought of the 1930s. Huge, cyclone-like winds, gathering speed from the west, often swept over us, sucking up our good soil and hurtling Russian Thistle and other small debris through the air, sometimes even lifting off a porch roof. Black dust clouds, roaring around us, turned day into night, but thankfully, we usually had enough warning to batten down the out-buildings before we rushed to the cellar to wait out the fury of the storm. It was a terrifying experience for a small child; only the quiet calmness of my parents kept me from breaking down. When the wind passed over, we trudged up from the basement to view the damage and to find the house full of dust.

One day, as I was coming home from school, in our horse-drawn school van, the driver pointed to the black clouds of a dust storm approaching from the northwest. I jumped out at our gate and flew to the house frantically calling for mother. Receiving no answer I ran to the barn. Dad wasn't there either. It was the first and only time I remember coming home from school and not finding at least one of my parents there, and it had to be on a day when this great storm was poised to strike!

Too frightened to go into the basement by myself — I think I thought the house might fall on me — I stood in the parched yard, my small heart pounding wildly and my bony knees trembling, watching those huge black clouds roll ever closer to our farm, which was right in their path. I closed my eyes tightly and prayed with childish fervour, "Oh, please God, help me!"

I'm not sure how long I stood with my eyes shut tight, waiting for the winds to bowl down on me, but when I did open them I was in for a wonderful surprise. The wind had changed its course, turning to the northeast, and those great dust clouds didn't touch our farm. It was so still I could hear the thumping of my heart. My shaking knees almost let me down as an awesome thought struck me — God had sent a sign that He'd heard the prayer of a frightened little girl.

But it faded from my memory, and when I grew up I scoffed at people who claimed to hear directly from God. I confess I'm still sceptical when someone tells me, "God spoke to me and told me to do such and such." Sometimes, it's just our own strong desires or wills that speak to us and not God at all.

A friend once informed me that God had told her to point out the faults of another woman in her church. She did, but in such an unloving, hurtful way that it completely shattered the other person. Surely God didn't tell her to do that! We must be careful about what we claim to be God's directives, and I am as positive as I am of day and night that He never sends us directions to hurt or abuse anyone, either with words or actions. He is much more likely to reveal His loving assurance and support.

One sleepless night when my husband and I were worried sick about a step one of our children was determined to take, I got up from my bed and wandered into the family room. Art and I had recently returned from a trip to England, and lying on the coffee table was a small book of prayers I had picked up in one of the cathedrals. It had never been read, but that night, I picked it up and cracked it open. The words from John 14 leapt out at me. "Let not your hearts be troubled, neither let them be afraid." These were familiar words, words I'd heard or read many times, but never had they spoken to me as they did that night. A wave of peace washed away all my fears, and I knew without any doubts that everything was going to be all right, even though I couldn't possibly see how.

Amazingly, the next morning brought a telephone call that changed the whole course of events. God moved into that situation so that all would, eventually, be well, well in a way we couldn't have imagined at that time.

It would be wonderful to say God gives me signs all the time, for everything. Not so. And this is often very perplexing to the believer. Why does God seem to speak so plainly on one occasion and withhold any indication He's remotely interested in our affairs another time? Every Christian I know speaks of 'dry' periods when God is silent, and prayers seem to bounce back from the ceiling. Interestingly, C.S. Lewis in his *Screwtape Letters* says that it's during these low periods (he calls them troughs) that our prayers mean the most to God — probably because it takes more faith to pray them.

It's easy to pray and believe when everything fits together in our lives, when we can do no wrong, when we feel we're living under God's grace. It's much harder to believe when events, and even people, turn against us, when no one seems to hear us, not even God. James Taylor in his book *Two Worlds in One* (Wood Lake Books, 1980) says it's like sitting by yourself on the bottom step of life. Nevertheless, it's on that bottom step where we learn the deeper things.

Being an impatient person, I have, for most of my life, prayed for patience in dealing with trying people and hard situations. Looking back, I can see how God answers that prayer by making me wait on that bottom step for long periods of time, often in the dark.

We live in a 'quick-fix' society, and we would like God to snap His fingers and fix our faults and woes immediately. As someone else has said, we want to live short-term lives in the service of a long-term God. A long interval may occur between an event in our lives and the unfolding of its purpose, but God's timing is never off.

It's also possible we may have to make some changes in our attitudes before God can answer our prayers. I may have to forgive someone, or more likely, ask someone to forgive me, especially if I'm asking God for patience. But however long the process, it's where I learn and grow.

The Book of Job is dear to my heart because it was the first book of the Bible I ever studied with a group. We were all novices and knew nothing about proper Bible study methods. Nevertheless, God was with us in our innocence and lack of knowledge, and that winter we learned many things from old Job. Since then, I often picture God and Satan meeting, and God asking, "Have you noticed my servant Gwyn, how she's doing so much better lately?" And Satan replying, "Well, yes, but you've been very good to her, blessing her at every chance. Just let me have a go at her and we'll soon see how well she's doing!" And God, smiling, steps aside and says, "Be my guest."

Well, of course you know what happens. The roof falls in at a place I thought I had patched up permanently, but which proves still to be very weak. Troubles pour in, and days of grace seem far away. But if, like Job, I can hang on through the deluge, God blesses me with deeper wisdom and moves me further along in my faith and understanding.

Another of my on-going prayers is that God will snuff out my pride, which is truly a most dreadful sin. He doesn't answer that prayer when my books are selling well, or when friends pat me on the back for some other small success. No, He answers that prayer in the experience of stinging humiliation when I do something very stupid and make a fool of myself, just when I thought I was being so clever. Now, if I allow Satan to use that humiliation, I will be cast down in despair, but if I give the experience over to God, I begin to see the humour in it, take myself much less seriously, and start to lose some of my pride.

Where do we learn courage and goodness and faith? Not at the top of the ladder where we're being hailed a success, but in situations where we must dig in and carry on, when we have to get up off that bottom step and start groping the long weary way to the top, even though we may not be able to see the way.

Jesus' critics asked Him to show them a sign to prove to them who He really was. He refused to do it, intimating that the only sign they needed was the fact that He was there. And so it is with us. He's there in the good times when His loving grace flows around us, but even more important, He's there when we're overwhelmed with disappointment or sorrow, supporting and strengthening us.

It takes faith to believe He sometimes does send us signs and miracles, but it takes a stronger faith to know He sits with us on the bottom-step days of our lives when, with His help, we find our way out of the blackness that surrounds us.

The point is we must keep in touch with God. I recall being shocked when two Protestant ministers, attending the same retreat as I, confessed to rarely praying outside the pulpit. I thought that was terribly remiss. I know old saints like Brother Lawrence, and some modern ones too, live so close to God their every breath is a prayer. Perhaps I should give my minister friends the benefit of the doubt, but I'm not sure that was the case with them. Most of us, even if we never breathe another prayer, are at least driven to recite the prayer, "Lord, have mercy on me, a sinner." For myself, there are many days I have to repeat it several times.

I threaded a ribbon through the hole in the stone I picked up on the beach the day we bought our lot and wore it to remind me that God does hear our prayers and answers in mysterious and wonderful ways. Eventually, however, I gave it away to someone else who needed to be reminded of that too.

For many years I looked for another stone with a hole through it but failed to find one. I did, however, gather a great collection of other stones.

PRECIOUS STONES

Chapter VII

Sometimes when I consider all the good friends who play such an important role in my life, I think of them as gems — diamonds, emeralds, topazes — each one with its own unique qualities and priceless value. Every one irreplaceable.

Of course, there are no precious stones on our beach, but there are many bits of coloured glass to remind me of them. Freshly broken glass is a scourge to any shoreline, so we are on a constant lookout to remove it from the path of tender feet.

However, when the glass is subjected to years of sloshing around in the water and sand, all the sharp edges wear smooth, and some talented people collect these lovely fragments of beach glass to make mosaics or jewellery.

Every time I see a piece of green glass in the sand and bend to pick it up, memories of my dear friend Kathleen wash over me. She was an ardent swimmer, and one day when she came to the beach, she removed her beautiful engagement ring, a square-cut emerald set with diamonds, and stowed it carefully in her shoe before she plunged into the lake. Finishing her swim, she dried herself off, and carelessly knocked the sand out of her shoes before hurrying home. Later, when washing the dishes, she missed her ring. Panic stricken, she returned to the beach to begin the frantic search — but hours of sifting and digging up sand revealed nothing. Dejected, she returned home without her precious ring. I promised I'd look for it every time I went to the beach; fifteen years later, my eyes still search for a glimpse of that priceless emerald.

Kathleen died twelve years ago, and on that day a light went out in the world. Irish, witty, dynamic, she never just walked into a room, but blew in, clearing out all gloom and bringing in gusts of good cheer and infectious laughter. Her sparkling blue eyes and wide smile invited everyone to laugh along with her, and it always gave me a lift to see her wheeling up to my back door on her bike, bringing a funny story or just some good, common sense spoken in her lilting Irish brogue.

Sometimes, she'd invite me for a walk, and I remember one day while we hiked along it began to rain. When I complained about getting wet, she laughed, "Don't worry, Gwyn, you won't melt — you're not made of sugar!" Ever since, rainy walks bring back her smile and words.

She was a 'born Christian' so there was never any need for her to be 'born again.' Her faith in God was vibrant and unshakable. She loved life, and by her own admission was a 'walking miracle,' but she never forgot it was God who made it so.

The seventh and last child of Northern Irish parents, she entered this world as a deformed weakling, with all her lower organs outside her body. The horrified doctor shook his head in dismay, "This child won't survive more than a few hours," he told the distraught parents.

Kathleen's mother and father could scarcely believe this tragedy. Their other six children were all born sound and healthy, and the mother's last confinement was normal in every way, indicating no abnormalities with the baby. They believed every child was a gift from God to be cherished and nurtured lovingly.

This thought sustained them, and they determined, regardless of the doctor's dismal outlook, to do everything possible to keep the little one alive. With unadulterated love and fervent prayer, they willed her to live through the first crucial hours. The hours crept into days, the days into weeks.

When she survived to six weeks, the astonished doctors exclaimed, "It's a miracle!" and decided to attempt the first of two delicate operations to place the organs inside the body. The tiny baby survived the first, to undergo the second operation when she was two. Although her condition improved somewhat, she was still small and weak, looking more like a white china doll than a baby.

Kathleen's parents were not wealthy, but they spared no expense to contact many eminent specialists who always gave them the same verdict: the child's bladder was completely useless and could never be repaired. Because she had no control, she was doomed to wear diapers and pads all her life, and furthermore, since she had no vagina, intercourse and childbearing were impossible. Not that this was of much concern since the doctors all predicted she wouldn't live past five years of age.

Yet the wee thing struggled on, showing a remarkable will to live in spite of contracting every ailment that came along — bronchitis, measles, chicken pox, and jaundice. When she was four, diphtheria struck her down again, and once more, the doctor shook his head sadly, "She'll slip away before morning."

But her faithful, praying parents held her in their arms the whole night through, again willing her to live. Next morning, when the doctor discovered she had not only survived the night, but was much improved, he could only exclaim, "It's a miracle."

The next prognosis was that she couldn't survive puberty but it, too, was reached and passed over. Actually, at this age Kathleen's health showed marked improvement. She attended school regularly, and her family encouraged her to lead as normal a life as possible while they constantly searched for better-designed, waterproof garments to conceal the embarrassing affliction that not even her closest friends knew about it.

She loved sports, and played for the tennis, field hockey, and badminton school teams. A natural in the water, she became a strong and swift swimmer, and she loved to bike through the lovely Irish countryside with her friends. She always recalled her teenage years as happy and fun-filled.

Older brothers and sisters married and moved away, but although Kathleen had some attentive beaus, she took none of them seriously because her mother had explained early, and as gently as possible, why Kathleen could never marry. Still, life seemed good to the young girl.

Then suddenly, when she was seventeen, her father died of a heart attack. Stricken with grief, she wondered if she could survive without his constant love and support, but she was

young, and her life stretched out ahead. She believed with all
her heart that God had a plan for her life, and she decided to live
one day at a time until He revealed it to her.

It began to unfold at the beginning of World War II.
George, a handsome young officer in Bomber Command, fell
deeply in love with her, and she with him. Because life was so
uncertain, he urged that they marry as soon as possible.

Kathleen confided to me, years later, that never, before or
after, had she endured such pain as when she tried to explain to
him the handicap that sentenced her to an unmarried state for
life. It took all the courage she could muster, but it had to be
done. Afterwards, she buried her head in his shoulder and wept.

While this must have been a terrible shock to George, he
dried her tears and convinced her she was the only girl he could
ever love. Bit by bit, he persuaded her his devotion went far
beyond the physical, that he still wanted to marry her. Her
mother, however, wouldn't hear of it. "It just can't be, Kathleen," she scolded. "It just can't be."

Eventually, George persuaded even her to give her reluctant consent. Nevertheless, she insisted they wait one year,
giving them time to rethink this momentous decision.

The year passed quickly, bringing the happy wedding day,
which in the past, Kathleen hadn't dared even dream about. "It
was like heaven come true," she recounted to me. "Truly, my
cup did run over."

George's leaves from the air force, though seldom and
short, were idyllic as they shared their love for one another. Yet,
nagging doubts kept creeping into her mind, "Could such a
marriage last?"

Within a year of their wedding, Kathleen learned of a
famous surgeon in Belfast with the reputation of accepting even
the most challenging and hopeless cases. A friend of a friend
knew him personally, and before long she wangled an introduc-
tion. She explained her condition while he listened with quiet
understanding. In less than two weeks she found herself in his
clinic undergoing tests to determine whether or not her kidneys
could withstand the implanting of an ureter, a tube to bypass the
useless bladder and lead directly into the bowel.

This procedure had only been attempted on wounded soldiers and many of them died during the operation. It was very risky, with a great danger of infection, but Kathleen knew the risk had to be taken, and said she reckoned if God could make the universe, He could certainly help the doctors remake her! After six hours, the operation came to a successful conclusion; a ureter was implanted from the kidneys to the bowel. Four months later, the useless bladder was removed, and still later, a famed gynaecologist built a vagina with an opening to the uterus which would allow normal intercourse.

After months in the hospital, Kathleen finally returned to her parents' home. For the first time in her life, her mother witnessed the morning when her darling daughter awoke to a dry bed. Seeing her deep prayers answered in a more marvellous way than she could imagine, she wept, "It's a miracle."

After the war, Kathleen and George immigrated to Canada where he became an Anglican priest. They adopted two lovely, healthy children and lived a full and happy life together for many years.

Kathleen continued to amaze doctors up to her dying day. Whenever she was in hospital, as she sometimes was, she was X-rayed and examined so young doctors could observe the miraculous medical process that kept her body functioning.

She taught me many things. It was impossible to be with her without sharing her compassion for all handicapped children and their parents. She knew firsthand about the sadness and despair, but also about the courage, strength, and dreams. She deplored and fought against decisions to allow, or even assist, some of these children to die in infancy because she believed, regardless of the handicap, life was a gift from God and therefore precious.

Many times I attended evensong or morning prayers at her church as she guided me through the Common Book of Prayer, until I grew to love the depth and breadth of the Anglican service. As a child, Kathleen committed passages of the Bible to memory and could quote me a psalm or verse to fit any occasion. Her faith in the goodness of God never wavered, and she said her earliest memory was of loving Him.

When I was still just a beginner in discovering the Bible, she persuaded me to subscribe to Scripture Union's *Daily Notes* which she'd read every day since a teenager. "It'll get you through the Bible in five years," she assured me. If that assessment is correct, I've covered the Bible several times, thanks to Kathleen!

She knew she had inherited a weak heart, her father and two brothers having died in their early fifties from heart attacks, but it didn't stop her from enjoying life to the maximum — swimming, golfing, biking, helping her husband in church work and conducting a community Bible study group up until her last days.

When she was sixty, she suffered a massive heart attack that nearly killed her. "When I lay there so sick, knowing I might die at any moment, the one hundred and fifteenth Psalm kept going through my head 'The Lord is not praised by the dead . . . but we, the living, will bless Him for evermore!'" She told me, "I asked God to spare my life so I could continue to praise Him."

And spare her He did — for awhile. As she had so often in her childhood, she defied the doctors' predictions and soon sprang back to her usual activities, perhaps not with the old vigour, but certainly with the same enthusiasm, always singing and laughing as she went along. Still, she knew her life was precarious.

Less than a year later, another heart attack struck her down, and this time, her laughing eyes, happy smile, and lovely lilting voice were gone forever. Yet we could do nothing less than celebrate a life that had shown so much courage and love.

Now, when I walk on the beach and bend to pick up a bit of emerald green glass, I often feel Kathleen walking with me, her eyes shining, her laughter lifting to the wind at the sheer joy of God's goodness. The one hundred and fifteenth Psalm says the dead can't praise God, but Kathleen is not dead. Her spirit lives, and somewhere she is among those who possess a life filled with joy and peace, experiencing, face to face, that amazing grace she so often sang about, "with no less days to sing God's praise than when we first began!"

Kathleen came into my life in my middle years, and although I knew her for less that twelve years, her friendship affected me profoundly.

Some of my friends I have known all my life, so nothing about me is hidden from them; others joined me along the way, right up until this year when I made two new ones. Each has a special place. It's nothing short of miraculous how God brings friends to us, weaving the threads of our lives together — sometimes loosely and not for long — other times tightly and for life!

Every friendship enriches and enlarges my life. Some friends offer their insights about God, helping me to expand my own; others bring comfort to soothe my soul when it's troubled. Still others come with holy laughter, dispelling depression. There are those who either trust or succour me as we share our innermost doubts and hopes, our fears and joys, our successes and disappointments.

Waldo Emerson made the famous pronouncement: "The only way to have a friend is to be one," but it's no small accomplishment to make a friend, and there's always risk. A woman I know went out of her way to befriend a woman in her apartment building, only to be savagely rebuffed. Then, too, there is much to give and take; my friends allow for lapses, and put up with the blemishes on my character so that I no longer have to pretend to be better or smarter than I am!

There can be no friendship, however, when one party contrives to get more out of it than the other. Although it is true that, at certain times, one friend may be called on to give more, each knows in her heart if the roles were reversed, the other would be just as kind. When I supported a friend through a devastating divorce, she said gratefully, "I hope you know, Gwyn, I'd do the same for you if you were in my position." Of course, I knew!

In a previous chapter, I mentioned how gratifying it is when one's children grow up to become one's friends. Still, we cannot rely on our children to be our only, or even our main source of physical and emotional bolstering. They are occupied with fulfilling their own destinies, and often, while we parents are still dancing to the old tune, they're moving to the sound of new music, leaving us out of step. No one can replace family when grief surrounds us, or when joyful occasions are celebrated, but on a day-to-day basis, it's our good friends who uphold us.

There are some things one can only share with a friend who will listen and not be shocked or pass judgement. There are always inequalities in families: a mother may favour a younger child while allotting too much responsibility to an older one; a father may demand perfection from one daughter, but pretend to lose a tennis match to another. With friends, however, the playing field is level and fair.

It's friendship that gives us a sense of individuality and significance, not as a mother's daughter, or a husband's wife, or a sister's pale shadow, but as a *chosen* companion in spite of our weaknesses. When we cannot accept those imperfections, when we demand more than a friend can give, or are jealous of his or her talents, the friendship dissipates into mere acquaintanceship.

What bonds me to my friends is 'kindredness,' a kind of spiritual recognition that here is someone who will share and sympathize with my deepest feelings and interests. Anne Shirley in *Anne of Green Gables* understood the importance of 'kinship.' She was always on the lookout for a 'kindred' spirit.

When I first walked into Joyce's house I wasn't looking for a friend, but almost immediately, something flickered between our souls that blithely announced "kindred spirits!"

I was drawn to her, first, because of our shared interest in old china and coloured glass, but even more because of her dry wit and open, warm friendliness. There was no pretence or putting on of airs with Joyce — what you saw was what you got, and I loved her frankness and honesty.

We first met when I worked for the newspaper, and arranged to do a photo-feature about her extensive collection of antiques, some of which were very rare and valuable.Nothing delighted Joyce more than to discover a piece of derelict furniture, scrape off all the layers of varnish or paint, repair and refinish it, and turn it into a thing of lasting beauty. Her spacious house was an antique lover's dream with its glowing furniture; every corner held an old cupboard brimmed full with china and glass. Worn, but lovely Persian or braided rugs covered the wood floors, adding warmth to every room. Her large collection of 'fairy' lamps shone in the sunlight streaming through a large window. It was a house filled with light and beauty.

As a result of that interview Joyce and I became good friends, attending auction sales together and searching out furniture for the house Art and I were already planning to build at the lake. We also appreciated her husband Nelson, and their ten-year-old niece, Brenda, whom they were raising because her mother died tragically when Brenda was an infant. This dear little girl was their pride and joy.

Two years after we met, Joyce, who was naturally thin and wiry, began to lose weight at an alarming rate and feel increasingly tired. She tried to laugh it off, "Just getting old, I guess." Finally, her doctor referred her to a specialist who pronounced the savage verdict of advanced leukemia, giving her only a few months to live.

The blow staggered her, but never floored her. She had deep sources of grit and determination, and soon she was reading every book she could find on the disease and contacting specialists all across the continent for advice. In her customary manner, she took control, placed herself on a special diet of herbs and sprouts with a high intake of vitamins and minerals. All the while she was undergoing a series of chemotherapy treatments at the cancer clinic in London.

Like Kathleen, she was an Anglican all her life, but although she was a regular, active church attender, she had never come up against anything like this before to test her faith. That faith grew all through her illness as she spent hours reading the Bible, especially the accounts of Jesus healing the sick.

She was well-loved in the community and highly esteemed among her teaching peers so she had many friends to support her in every way. There were, however, only two or three with whom she felt comfortable enough to speak to about God and praying with her.

"I *know* it's not God's will for me to die," she insisted. "If I just have enough faith, He'll heal me — so, *please,* keep praying for me!"

We did, of course, even though we watched her losing ground. It became a concern that she would never consider the alternative to getting well. One day, as I accompanied her to the chemotherapy treatment clinic, I glanced over at her thin, jaundiced face, tense under the bright red paisley scarf she tied bravely around her head to hide her loss of hair. My heart ached, wanting so much for her to find peace. "Joyce," I asked gently, "can you place your life in God's hand, no matter what happens?" and I quoted from Paul's Letter to the Romans, ending with, "Whether we live or die we belong to God." I asked again, "Can you believe, even if you don't get well, God will still look after you?"

"Gwyn," she answered firmly, "I know when I die I'll be in God's hands, but I just *can't* believe He wants me to die *now*. Why would He take Brenda's mother from her when she was a baby, and now take me, the only mother she's ever known? If He's a God of love and mercy, I just can't believe He'd do that!" Then she added, "I believe He's testing my faith, and I *need you* to believe that too!" What could I answer?

Driving home after the treatment, she turned to me again. "Gwyn, I want the laying-on-of-hands and prayer for healing." I agreed it was a good idea. Then she continued, "But I don't want my minister to do it because I know he wouldn't be comfortable about it or maybe wouldn't even believe in it. I want you to do it, with only Nelson, Art, Flora and Jack (other good friends) present.

There was nothing I wouldn't do for Joyce, but I did have reservations and asked if she had thought this through carefully. "I have," she answered with her usual steady look, "and I'm sure!"

After I got home, I pondered a good deal about what she had asked, reading and re-reading portions of the Bible dealing with healing, especially the Book of James. After discussing it with Jack and Flora and Art, an evening was arranged to meet at our house.

Joyce was buoyed up and expectant as we gathered around her. Jack read from the Bible, and then we all laid our hands on her head and shoulders and prayed for her healing. No more fervent prayers were ever sent heavenward. Nevertheless, she grew steadily worse.

A local man who suffered from a different kind of cancer visited Joyce to tell her about a faith healer in Flint, Michigan. He recounted seeing many alleged healings, and said he was going back for the next meeting. Although, by this time, she was very weak and sick, Joyce decided to make that trip too. As she lay on pillows in the back seat of the car, Nelson drove her the hundred and twenty miles, followed by another car carrying friends.

We arrived early, but even then throngs of people were streaming into the huge auditorium. Many were on crutches or in wheelchairs, but everyone was striving to get in before the place filled up and the doors closed. Art found seats for Joyce and Nelson up near the front, while the rest of us sat in the balcony.

I had attended a few healing services before — one in an Anglican church in Toronto and another in a small country church, led by Dr. Albert Cliffe, an Anglican scientist/lay preacher whose prayers and touch brought healing to many people in the 1960s.

On another occasion, my friend Molly and I joined a group going by bus to a service at the London Gardens where the evangelist-healer Kathryn Kuhlman conducted a service. The place was packed to the rafters, and though we were far up in the stands, we witnessed hundreds of folk streaming up the aisles to be prayed for by Kathryn. She was very dramatic in her long, flowing white robes and pretty with her golden hair and willowy figure. Still, it was hard not to believe she had some kind of special gift beyond explanation. Two years later, while on a holiday in Bermuda, I met a man who, in the course of our conversation, mentioned he had been healed of a serious back problem at that Kuhlman service in London, furthering my belief that God does, sometimes, heal people in a miraculous way.

In Flint the young evangelist bounded out on stage, dressed in a white suit, several large rings glittering on his fingers. He was short but quite handsome with his black hair and flashing eyes. Striding around on the stage like a barker from a circus, he soon had the audience mesmerized. Many people, struggling to get their ailing loved ones up on stage were held back by

ushers. Those who did reach the front were prayed over and
touched lightly on the forehead. Several were 'slain in the
spirit,' that strange phenomenon that causes people to fall
limply to the floor, seeming to lose consciousness for several
minutes.

Large collection baskets were passed several times as
ushers moved through the audience selling photographs of the
evangelist or copies of his many tape recordings. At times it
really did appear more like a circus than a healing service.

"How many here love God?" demanded the young man in
white, as he bounced around on the stage. "Put up your hands!"
Who of us was going to leave them down?

"How many love God enough to give Him a hundred
dollars?" Hundreds of hands shot up, and the baskets were
passed.

"How many love Him enough to give fifty dollars?" More
hands waved, and again the baskets went around.

As so it went, right down to loving God five dollars worth.

Two hours after it opened, the meeting closed abruptly. Our
healer strode off the stage with no backward look, leaving
dozens of disappointed sick folk who never made it up to the
stage for his prayer or touch. As we poured out of the building,
another throng surged forward to take our places for yet another
healing service. One can only imagine what the financial take
was for that evening.

We were angry and deeply ashamed that such a meeting
could be held in the name of Christ. People who are very ill, or
have dear ones threatened by death are vulnerable and very apt
to fall prey to the scurrilous claims of the fraudulent. We didn't
discuss it much afterwards except for Joyce who said, "Well, it
didn't do me any harm, and it *may* have done me some good."

Her good days became fewer and fewer, but she was never
hospitalized because Nelson arranged for health care workers
to look after her at home. Her last days were spent in her
pleasant upstairs bedroom where she continued to greet friends
with a brave smile.

The last time I visited her she was in deep distress. So frail,
with her face screwed up in pain, she seethed through clenched

teeth, "Damn you, God, if You're so determined to take me, why don't You take me *NOW!*

I held her small, thin hand and stroked her forehead. Tears seeped through her closed lids, "I'm sorry," she whispered, "that was a terrible thing to say." Then opening her eyes wide she said, "Gwyn, I still believe God is going to heal me." Two days later she died.

We were numb — numb with grief because we lost such a dear person, but also because we felt something was left unfinished, that Joyce hadn't been able to relinquish her life and find peace before she died.

The funeral was large, friends coming from all over the province and filling the church to its limits. I recall nothing of the service except that at the end as we filed out, slowly following the casket, mighty chords began to pour from the organ. I stopped — searching for the words to fit the music that rolled around us like thunder. Then they came —

"When peace, like a river, attendeth my way
When sorrows like sea-billows roll;
Whatever my way, Thou has taught me to say,
It is well, it is well with my soul.
I had to believe Joyce had found peace at last.

Nevertheless, many perplexing questions remained. Why, for instance, do some people receive miraculous healing while others do not, even though, as with Joyce, their faith is strong? Why are some devoured slowly by excruciating illnesses, when others seem to slip out so easily and quietly? What is the use or value of suffering?

I was also deeply troubled about the laying-on-of-hands and prayer we had for Joyce at our home. I castigated myself for not insisting on an ordained minister being present. Was it, I agonized, because it secretly pleased me that Joyce had wanted me to do it? Was it *my* pride that got in the way of *her* healing?

Time and again I went back to reread The Book of Job, to learn something more about being humble before God. Like Job, I had to concede that while there are many things which we cannot understand in both the physical and spiritual realms, it is enough for us to know that God is the Supreme Creator. God, our great and powerful Friend, requires none of our feeble efforts in fulfilling His 'manifold' and 'righteous' works, whether they be healing, giving, or taking life.

He has blessed me with many friends. All are special, but my Christian friends are especially dear. Every spring I go on a three-day retreat with a group of other Christian women, and we enjoy such a beautiful time of being apart from the world with all its busyness that it's difficult to put into words what it really means to us. It's true we're charmed by the old stone house we rent every year, so that it's always like coming home when we walk through the door. It's also true that we love the hiking trails and the heady scent of pine and cedar along the way, and we do gain much from the Bible study led by one of the group. But while all of these make our time together special, what makes it *extra* special is the fellowship with the other women. In this day and age of inclusive language, I smile at the use of the word 'fellowship,' and I struggle to find another, but cannot. It *is* the fellowship — the *being with,* not just in body but in spirit; it is coming from and appreciating the same Christian perspective that goes far beyond a word like companionship, for instance. In talking openly, in listening attentively, in empathizing, in consoling, and in laughing joyfully, we feel we are all part of the family of God.

An unknown poet said, "Every true friend is a glimpse of God." As I hold in my hand some pieces of brightly coloured beach glass which remind me of my varied precious friends, I thank Him for all the glimpses He has given me through them.

THE LONE STONES

Chapter VIII

Sometimes, when a storm blows over the Lake, the waves pound on the shore, heaving in tons of sand to cover all the small stones. Before the sand is dragged back to the water, the stones hide under this rippled blanket of sand; only one or two large ones stand above like sentinels keeping watch. Somehow, these lone stones remind me of ministers of the church, the shepherds who often stand alone while leading and guarding their flocks. I thank God for those who have guarded and helped me.

Thus far, I've spoken mostly about the women who nurtured my faith, but there were many men too. The first, of course, was my father Alex. His Christian faith was unchanging and steady. Not well-schooled, having only completed Grade eight, his speech wasn't always grammatically correct nor his vocabulary extensive, yet he expressed his faith in the same manner that he lived every day of his life. Honest, kind, true, he always forgave his children's foolishness and gave them another chance to prove themselves. When I was little I thought he had a special line to God, and I was comforted when I walked by his bedroom and saw him kneeling in prayer at his bedside.

If I thought I knew where my father stood with God, I was never sure about my mother. She didn't kneel for prayer, although she assured me she *did* pray and often with her eyes wide open! She was very suspicious of people who wore their religion on their sleeves — especially Bible-quoting ones. Her doubts were substantiated by my paternal grandfather who carried his Bible under his arm, quoted from it effusively, and rose in his pew in church to argue a point with the minister right on the spot. He may have been a Christian, but he was also an irregular, difficult person with a temper that flared up instantaneously burning anyone nearby. Mother had no patience with him at all, and in an indirect way, my reaction to certain Christians has been tempered by her view of my grandfather.

So different from his father, my dad was gentle and even-tempered. Using him as a model, his children didn't find it difficult to view God as a loving heavenly Father, although I know now how difficult that is for those who've had hard, impatient fathers. I was fortunate, indeed, to be blessed with a dad who started me on my Christian journey from the day I was born.

Of course, my husband Art has been an important guide, too, even though we practice our religion quite differently. He's a quiet man, keeping what goes on between him and God private. Yet, he is strong in his faith, and sometimes when I get a little out of kilter in my enthusiasm, he acts as an excellent plumb line to keep me straight.

Several ministers of the church helped guide me, but I'm especially indebted to four — the Reverends Donald Sinclair, Samuel Kerr, John Boyne, and Wilfred (Biff) Jarvis.

When Art and I first married and lived in Toronto, we went to church only sporadically. After we moved back to Exeter, it seemed reasonable to me that we attend the United Church of Canada where I was still a member. Art was just as adamant that we go to the Presbyterian Church, and since we couldn't agree, we didn't attend church at all.

One day when I was down on my knees scrubbing the floor, dressed in the skimpiest shorts and halter-top, a soft knock came to the door. I opened it to find a strange, shy-looking young man who turned out to be the new Presbyterian minister! Embarrassed at my lack of proper wearing apparel, I nevertheless, invited him in, quickly changed my clothes, and sat down to chat. In a few moments he put me at ease with his dry sense of humour, and since he was a bachelor, I asked him to stay on for supper. He and Art and I had a wonderful evening together.

Shortly after, he brought his bride Helen to the manse, and the four of us became life-long friends. Under Don's guidance, we also became life-long Presbyterians, joining the local membership and taking on offices in the congregation.

I think Helen and Don were the first Christians I'd met who wore their Christianity with such a sense of fun and joy. Their faith was certainly no burden; in fact, they seemed to actually *enjoy* it! Not much wonder we were attracted and wanted to emulate them as much as possible. Thus it was that Don and Helen started me walking from the place in my faith where I'd been sitting since I was a child.

Next came the Reverend Sam Kerr, an Irishman with a very peculiar brogue. Sam was much older than Don Sinclair, a well-seasoned man of God, and a gentleman in every sense of the word. Dead serious about the faith, he too had a twinkle in his eye and a story for every occasion. And he was very wise, listening to me and straightening me out more than once. One time when I became upset because I thought the women of the congregation were spending too much time catering to banquets and not enough on the welfare of their souls, I spoke to him about it. Stretching his legs out in front of him, he fixed me with his twinkle and drawled, "Oh, I don't know, Gwyn, those bun feeds aren't all bad — it's a chance for some of those women to give their talents to the church while bonding them together with Christian love."

Sam Kerr was kindness personified, always sensing someone's unhappiness and smoothing it over. At age six, Robert had four lines to say at the Christmas concert, and was so excited he left for the church before the rest of us finished supper. While he helped Mr. Kerr arrange the chairs, he recited his lines, over and over, making sure he knew them perfectly.

Finally, the big moment came. Striding confidently out on the stage, he faced the audience and was suddenly tongue-tied. Seeing him squirming, Mr. Kerr strolled up quietly beside him, put his arm around his small shoulders and scolded the audience, "You people have just gone and scared Robert; he knows his piece perfectly, so he does!" Then, cuing the small boy at his side, they recited the lines together. Any mother would love a minister like that!

Mr. Kerr held Sunday evening discussions, covering everything from reincarnation to the possibility of life in space, all viewed from the basis of our Christian faith. He made us probe and think, while admitting he still had many unanswered questions himself. This was a great revelation (and comfort) to me; until then I supposed ministers knew all the answers!

After five years it was sad to see Mr. Kerr leave our congregation, but we looked forward to another young minister — just a few years out of college, idealistic, and very serious came the Reverend John Boyne. No one went to sleep during John's sermons. He might sometimes scorch our ears with his language, but he always held our attention and got his point across. Even today, I recall some of his sermons that touched the bone. To him I owe a special debt and not just for his preaching.

By the time he arrived, I was very involved with church work — leader of the CGIT, superintendent of the Sunday School, member of the board of managers, and president of the women's group. Because it was a small congregation, many members filled several positions so I was not particularly unique. However, the day came when I began to wonder what all this running around accomplished, and to doubt the validity of my faith. Suspicious that I was play-acting, pretending to be a Christian when all the while there seemed no depth or meaning to my life. I felt that those friends who never attended church or wanted any part of it were more honest than I who jumped through all the right holy hoops but didn't know why. After searching my soul, I concluded I had to find out if there really was something to being a Christian or give it all up as a myth as the sceptics assured me it was!

I poured out all my doubts to Jack Boyne who, surprisingly, confided he had gone through much the same turmoil before he accepted the call to the ministry. He suggested several books that he thought might help.

I can never thank him enough for introducing me to the writings of C.S. Lewis. I devoured everything I could find — *Surprised by Joy, Mere Christianity, The Great Divorce,* and many others. Lewis, himself, had started out on a search — a search for the source of the haunting feelings of joy that came to him at unexpected moments. To his great surprise it led him to Christianity, making him one of its staunchest advocates. He was considered one of the English-speaking world's leading intellectuals and an authority on English literature, and although his search had been much different from mine in that he made a serious study of all the world's main religions, I was convinced that if a person of his genius could accept Christ as the source of strength and joy of his life, then I, who was anything but a genius, could too.

John Boyne suggested that I start teaching the young-adult Sunday School class. I flatly refused because I knew I wasn't equipped to teach those teenagers anything, let alone the Bible. John, however, wouldn't accept a refusal. "You'll learn along with them," he insisted. "And remember you don't have to teach them *everything*. Before they come to your class they will have already learned much from someone else, and after they leave they will still go on learning!" I finally agreed, and he loaded me up with the study guides. Opening them up at home, I discovered the first lesson was on "eschatology." I'd never even heard of the word. "Help," I phoned back to John. He laughed, "I'll teach this first lesson, but then, you're on your own!"

It turned out to be one of the best things I ever did. It's true I had to study hard and spend much time in preparation just to keep up with those smart young people, but my knowledge expanded in ways it might not have done otherwise. Besides our regular Sunday morning classes, we explored many avenues, including a Jewish synagogue where a friendly rabbi explained the Jewish faith which, of course, is the root of Christianity. We also received a pleasant welcome to a Muslim mosque where, again, we were given an exposition on Islam. We attended Catholic services, as well as several at other Protestant churches, coming back to discuss what we'd heard and learned. Some of the young people remained in that class five or six years, and I like to think it made a difference in, at least, some of their lives. I know it made a difference in mine. During those years of reading, studying, and teaching, my Christian faith became the most important element in my life.

When John Boyne left for a city church, Biff Jarvis came to our three-point charge, and it was during his ministry that I was ordained an elder. Biff and I didn't always agree, but we *always* respected each other. He supported me during Robert's difficult teenage years, adding his prayers to mine. In turn, I stood by him when he was confronted with open hostility at one of his churches. For several weeks, he and I met one morning a week for prayer. Even after more than fifteen years, he remains a special person to me.

And so do the other three. The twenty-odd years covered by those four ministers were the most important in my spiritual growth. I came to the point of giving my whole life over to God's will. There were no flashes of lightning, no Damascus Road experiences, just a steady climb to the truth, and the realization that Jesus Christ is, indeed, the Source of all my being. I owe much to the men who helped guide me on that climb.

Being a shepherd of the sheep is a privilege, but I've never heard one minister say it's easy. It's impossible to please everyone in the congregation no matter how hard one tries. Today, ministers are called upon to do a great deal more than preach and visit the sick; much of their time is spent counselling people with a large range of serious social ills. Their days are rarely their own, and they, and their families too, sacrifice much for their congregations. Most of us can find confidants to share our woes, but the poor minister hardly dares make a close friend for fear of offending someone else.

A recent phenomenon is support groups for 'abused' ministers. It's probably long overdue, but speaks shamefully of our Christian congregations who make too many demands on their ministers, while giving back too little love and understanding.

There's one more man-of-the-cloth I can't forget — one not of my own denomination, but a neighbour, the Reverend Ernest Lewis, who upheld me when no one else wanted to. It was due to my involvement with a residential nursing home nearby.

By this time, I was so enthusiastic about my faith, I longed to do *something* for God. Not particularly well-endowed with talents, I still felt I might be of use and every morning prayed He'd favour me with some small duty. I learned one has to be careful in asking God for a job because it may demand more than one expects.

Walking up town, one day, I passed the residential home for ex-psychiatric patients which had opened a few months before, and where all the residents were women in their middle to late years. Some of them had been hospitalized for decades, losing all contact with their families. With the advent of better drugs and changing government regulations, they were discharged with no place to go except a nursing home.

These women looked so forlorn, going out for their daily walk, looking like a flock of frightened sheep, scuttering down the street, clustering together, heads down, oblivious to everything and everyone. As I walked by on this particular day, I noticed most of the women sitting silently on the veranda, rocking back and forth and staring into space like lost souls. My heart was touched, and I wondered if I might do something for them.

Returning home, I phoned the owner to ask if one of her ladies would like to do some light housekeeping jobs for me to earn a bit of money. She said 'Marjory' would be happy to come, and it was arranged for me to go over and show her the way to my home.

A tall lady in her mid-fifties, Marjory, despite her illness, still had an air of elegance, carrying herself with nervous grace. Her movements, however, were quick and jerky and I soon learned not to let her wash my good dishes or dust my antiques. She loved to iron, which suited me fine since I hated the job myself. Marjory's presence at our house solved the problem of the ever-overflowing basket of unironed clothes.

In the beginning, she talked very little, but bit by bit, she began to tell me something of her life. The only child of doting parents, she often referred to 'mother,' who was still living, though very elderly. Marjory had been a teacher in a country school on the Bruce Peninsula, and from snatches of her memories I gathered she had travelled quite extensively. I wondered what had caused her mental breakdown, but she never gave me a hint. Not until several years later, when her mother died, did a friend relate Marjory's sad story at the funeral.

One day, just before Christmas, Marjory sent out two boys to cut down a Christmas tree in a nearby bush for the school concert. Without warning, a violent blizzard struck, blocking

out all visibility and dropping the temperature to thirty degrees
below zero. The boys never returned. When the storm abated, a
search party found their frozen bodies in the woods. Poor
Marjory, blaming herself for their tragic deaths, suffered a
breakdown from which she never fully recovered. Her father
had died, and her aging mother had no recourse but to commit
her to an asylum, where she stayed for years before being
released to the nursing home.

The ladies from the home all attended Reverend Lewis's
United Church which was close by, but one day, Marjory confessed she, too, was a Presbyterian and thereafter happily went
to church with us. She became part of our family, coming to us
for Christmas and birthday celebrations. A few times she invited
the other ladies over for a cup of tea, which pleased them all
even though they rarely lifted their downcast eyes.

Through Marjory I learned there was little social activity
in the home. Occasionally, one of the churches presented a short
concert,but nothing was organized on a day-to-day or even a
weekly basis. I also heard from Marjory that the administrator-
owner was sometimes 'nasty' with the ladies, but I made ex-
cuses for her, saying she was probably overworked and tired. I
wondered if I should try to help by organizing some kind of
activities for the residents.

I talked over the idea with Mr. Lewis when he was working
in his garden one day. "It's a capital idea," he exclaimed. "Those
poor women certainly need someone to put a bit of cheer in their
lives!" He assured me his church parlour would be available if
I could arrange some activities.

Encouraged by his support I hastened to visit the owner of
the home to broach the subject with her. She seemed delighted,
saying she was too busy just looking after all the residents'
physical comforts.

It was not difficult to find six friends to help organize a few
activities. We decided we'd meet with the ladies two mornings
a week in Mr. Lewis's church parlour for some music, games,
and simple crafts. The first few weeks were like being with the
walking dead. When the women spoke at all, it was in muffled
monosyllables, and they moved very awkwardly, standing or
sitting close together for support. Even Marjory, who carried on

a conversation when she was alone with me, reverted to being just like the others. Finally, we struck on playing bingo and little by little they began to come to life, because just like children they loved to win the prizes.

After two or three months, with some love and appreciation, those women bloomed like bright tulips bursting out after a long, cold winter. They were still subdued and sometimes even fearful when they first arrived each morning, but they soon began to smile and relax and take part in our activities. We learned some songs, played games, and did some easy crafts, such as covering coat hangers and making table decorations.

After several months we had enough goods to hold a bazaar and were delighted with the turnout of customers. Dressed up in their best, some of the ladies served tea and cookies to our guests, and they were beyond themselves with pleasure. The proceeds were divided equally among them, and because they had little or no spending money, they were as thrilled as if we'd handed them a million dollars.

As trust built up and we all became friends, the mantle of sadness covering them slowly lifted, but there remained a fearfulness that never left. Sometimes they'd arrive at the church parlour visibly upset, but when I questioned them, they just lowered their eyes and refused to speak until we moved on to bingo. My feelings grew more and more uneasy about how they were being treated at the home.

One morning when they trooped in we knew something terrible had happened. They moved like zombies or people under a spell, their muscles stiff, and faces filled with terror. "What's happened? What's the matter?" I kept asking as we tried to soothe and comfort them. Finally, Mrs. Heintz, who was always a little braver than the rest, began to tell us how the owner had flown into a rage when one of them upset her coffee on the breakfast table. In her anger she knocked two women off their chairs and flailed the rest with threatening, filthy language.

"Does this happen often?" I asked. "Often," Mrs. Heintz replied with tears welling up in her eyes. Taking her hand in mine I looked into her eyes, "It's going to be all right," I assured her. "I'll look into it."

She pulled her hand away. "No, no!" she cried, "Don't do anything. If she finds out I told you, I don't know what she'll do to us!" Some of the others joined in, begging me not to complain. The fear in their eyes spoke volumes.

I wrote a letter to the district supervisor, telling him what had happened and listing my worst fears. A young social worker came to visit me shortly after. He said he inspected the home once a month and while his inner feeling was that the residents were being mistreated, he could never get one of them to admit it.

"They're too terrified," I explained.

"Well," he replied, "document everything you can, and try to get something concrete because if it's only their word against hers not much can be done."

As we continued our twice-weekly sessions, the women's trust grew until they openly told of treatment that shocked me. The home with run an iron fist; no questions or complaints were allowed. Probably because they were on medication, they moved slowly and often awkwardly. When they moved too slowly they were pushed, sometimes knocked down. One day Marjory arrived at our house with large bruises on her arm and leg. "What happened?" I asked. "I was pushed down the stairs when I couldn't get out of way."

I phoned the owner — "I was wondering how Marjory got those bruises on her arm and leg?"

"You know perfectly well how awkward she is," she snapped. "She stumbled and fell down the stairs. It's a wonder she didn't break her neck."

Even worse than the physical abuse was the emotional and psychological stress. The treatment they received was degrading and inhuman. Every morning and afternoon they were locked out of the house for an hour or more. That wasn't so bad in the summertime when they could go to the park, but on the coldest days of winter, or the wettest days of spring, they were turned out. Often, the poor things huddled in a store or church doorway, like cattle in a fence corner with their backs to the storm.

Every week I sent off another letter to the district supervisor, recording my latest complaint, insisting the owner's license be revoked. Still nothing happened.

One cold, stormy day when the weather wasn't fit for anyone to be out, she sent them forth. "If it's too cold for you," she crowed, "go to your friend Mrs. Whilsmith. See if she'll take you in." I did, of course, and over hot tea and Christmas cake, they poured out their souls.

After months of listing my complaints against the owner, the supervisor still took no action. My young social worker friend told me it was because I didn't have enough hard evidence, and also because the supervisor had decided I was a neurotic trouble-maker!

Through all this frustration, the Reverend Lewis remained my constant sounding board and bulwark. He, too, wrote letters making his own charges, and assuring the supervisor of my integrity.

Finally, when I realized I was getting nowhere at the local level I wrote a letter to the Minister of Health at Queen's Park in Toronto. A polite reply informed me the matter would be dealt with. When two or three weeks passed with no action I wrote again — and again — and again.

A story appeared in the newspaper in which the owner pictured herself as a much-maligned victim of an unfounded attack, stressing her only desire was to provide a caring home for the residents. She ended the interview by saying she was contacting her lawyer and contemplating a libel suit against the victimizer (me). I laughed out loud, but my laughter didn't last long.

A few days later, Art and I had a visit from our Member of Parliament who was also a high-profile member of the cabinet at Queen's Park. He came, he said, as a friend (which he was) to caution me against pursuing my charges against the nursing home owner. The Minister of Health had spoken to him about the case and felt it would be very difficult to substantiate my claims of abuse, and that if the Ministry cleared Mrs. Bower's name, she would, in fact, have the fuel to light her libel charges against me. If she won, we might lose everything we owned.

This certainly sobered me. "Well," I asked Art, "what am I supposed to do now? You know as well as I do those women are being abused!" Art answered, "I guess you'll have to do whatever it is you have to do."

I was so thankful he didn't ask me to call off my campaign, I almost broke down and cried. Nevertheless, I knew it was a serious, and maybe even dangerous, road ahead. I desperately wanted someone with influence to travel it with me, but although almost everyone in town knew something of what went on in that home, no one would get involved — not the politicians, the business people, or anyone else.

I was positive one woman, one of the town's most influential citizens, would back me up; I asked her to write letters on my behalf and support me in trying to improve conditions at the home, but she replied, "I'm sorry I can't do that. I know you're sincere and that your charges are probably true, but because of my husband's position in this town, I just can't get involved."

Devastated, I left her house feeling depressed and alone, wondering if it was worth all the effort. As fate would have it, however, I met some of the ladies from the home on my way. They gathered around, so pleased to see me, treating me like a long-lost friend even though I had just seen them the day before. They had no idea of my turmoil, but when I looked at their dear faces, I knew I couldn't let them down.

Dropping in to see Mr. Lewis I told him of the Cabinet Minister's visit and my feelings of desolation. "You mustn't give up," he admonished me. "What you're doing is right. That license must be revoked. God is on our side! What we need to do now," he continued, "is keep on writing letters until somebody does something."

That's what we did — writing again to both the local supervisor and to the Ministry of Health in Toronto.

It paid off. One morning, soon after, the social worker phoned. "I'm not supposed to do this," he confided, "but I wanted to let you know that tomorrow both you and the home operator will receive surprise visits from the chief psychiatrist at the Ministry of Health."

Thankful as I was for that clandestine warning, it completely unnerved me. I knew that if I came across as a neurotic lunatic (as the local supervisor painted me) all was lost. I prayed fervently that I would be convincing and keep my composure. Next morning I awoke with hundreds of butterflies in my stomach until I remembered, *"This is the day I've been waiting for — the day someone from the Ministry is coming to inspect the home for himself."* My heart lifted as I thought out loud, "This is the day that the Lord has made; I will rejoice and be glad in it!"

The doctor arrived — a smiling, pleasant man. We sat in my living room discussing my accusations. I had kept a record of all the cruel treatment the ladies related to me. It was long and included Marjory being pushed downstairs and Mabel being sent to bed without supper because she dared say she didn't like a certain food on her plate. There was a record of the residents being shut outside for an hour in sub-zero weather, of their arms being pinched, and their hair pulled. And worst of all the vile verbal abuse that she heaped on them daily, humiliating and dehumanizing them.

The doctor looked over my list. "This is all very serious," he agreed, "but none of it can be substantiated. Can't you think of one thing that will prove, beyond a doubt, that the women are being abused?"

I racked my brain and then I remembered something. Three weeks before, I noticed Marjory wasn't wearing her prized wrist watch, a gift from her mother. When I asked her why, she replied, "Well, a few days ago when Mrs. ..... told us to go to bed, Mrs. Heintz pointed out that it was only seven o'clock. That made Mrs. ..... so angry she took all our wrist watches and locked them up. Then she removed all the clocks from the walls, so now we never know what time it is."

I turned to the doctor, "If those women's watches are still locked up, and if there are no clocks on the walls, will that substantiate my claims?" "It will," he replied.

Off he went, and I prayed the owner hadn't had a sudden change of heart and given the ladies back their watches. About an hour later he returned with a wide smile on his face. "You've been vindicated."

He recounted how he had been received graciously by the owner, but when he showed her my list of complaints (all except the one about the wrist watches) she hotly refuted them, saying she couldn't understand why Mrs. Whilsmith would make such wicked and untrue statements.

Then she escorted him through the house, pointing out all the good points, assuring him she only had the welfare of the residents at heart. Although he didn't speak at length to any of the women, he sensed their fear and discomfort. When he and the owner finished the tour he said, "Well, it seems you run a comfortable home, but there is something that puzzles me. I noticed that not one of the women is wearing a wrist watch. Surely some of them own watches, do they not?" She alleged that they did. "Please ask them to go to their rooms and get them for me."

Her face reddening, she admitted the watches weren't in their rooms, and when he pressed the matter further, she went to her wall safe and brought them out. Then he continued, "I also noticed there isn't one clock in this house. Do you not have any clocks?" Yes, she had clocks. Where? In a locked drawer.

Halleluja! The missing time-pieces were enough to prove cruel and unnecessary treatment and clench my case.

The license was not renewed and, thankfully, new young owners turned the nursing home from one of gloom and fear to one of light and happiness. They brought laughter, and tenderness, and life for the ladies changed overnight. Now, they were allowed to think for themselves, go up town if they wanted to or stay home if they felt like it, and make many other decisions for themselves. They blossomed under their new freedom, and the new owners introduced so many interesting programs for them, my friends and I were no longer needed to conduct morning sessions in the church parlour.

Two years before, when I asked God for some work to do for Him, I had no idea what He'd trust me with. For a few months, I was happy to believe it was just organizing a few pleasant diversions for those lonely ladies. His plans, however, were larger. I believe, as He looked down on those helpless, misused women, He was filled with great compassion to change the owner and administrator of that nursing home. There were days when I felt I couldn't see the task through, but because He is the foundation of our strength and because He provided Mr. Lewis to encourage me, the job got done.

During that period of standing alone, I learned something about what it means to be a 'lone stone' myself, and my appreciation for all ministers and priests and all others who take a stand for the Right, often against great opposition, increased manifold.

THE CROSS AND
CORNER STONE

Chapter IX

Seven months have passed since I began writing about my basket of stones last fall. November brought gale force winds beating across the water, whipping it up until it reared and frothed and spewed like a hundred roaring dragons gone amuck, as it thrashed angrily at the high clay cliffs.

We had snow for Christmas with all the family home and, somehow, it seemed more blessed than ever as we shared our human love while remembering God's great gift to us. We had all agreed beforehand to exchange only 'recycled' gifts, for which we paid nothing or very little, thus, eliminating worry and expense and having more funds to share with a local charity.

The gifts, in surprising shapes and sizes, were beautifully wrapped and piled in the decorated wicker clothes hamper beside the tree. Each person picked a number, and when our number was called we either chose a gift from the basket or 'stole' one from someone who had already opened a present. The gifts were unique, from a slightly damaged, but beautiful, enamelled bread tray to a frozen trout Robert had caught last fall, which kept being stolen by all the avid fish-eaters in the family!

In January the temperature dropped, and winds blasting in from the north stilled the great waves. Mountains of ice built up on shore until there was only an expanse of snow and ice as far as we could see. On still sunny days, it sparkled in the pale yellow sunshine like a soft white quilt studded with millions of diamonds.

Acquaintances often wonder why we stay the winter here. We like it; it's peaceful and quiet and there's time for writing or woodworking or the many other projects Art and I enjoy. Wood fires burn in the kitchen stove and in the downstairs fireplace, making us as cosy and warm as two bears in hibernation. Friends, not far away, come for long lunches or invite us to their houses for games of Probe.

Nevertheless, we anticipate the arrival of March, and watch from our windows as the lake becomes a battle ground, winter and spring the adversaries. Premature warm days cause chinks in the thick ice, but winter, never giving up easily, dips the temperature again and heaves in more snow. Still, spring persists, and in a few days a strip of blue water appears on the horizon. The next day, winter closes it up, and so it goes, back and forth. Eventually, a wind from the east blows the blanket of ice far out into the lake. Winter may send a final blustery northwester to shove it back to shore, but it's a losing battle, and although the fight may go on for several weeks, winter finally retreats leaving the lake in her shimmering mantle of blue to spring.

The middle of March brings back the tundra swans winging their way northward. Following infallible instincts, they fly the same route every spring, and on their way stop over in our area for rest and food. Every night, for at least two weeks, we marvel as they fly low over our house in wave after wave, coming from the fields where they feed, to settle on the lake for the night, their excited gabbling going on into the wee hours.

Just as they come, they leave, flying off one morning to complete the journey that takes them on for hundreds of miles, to summer in the Arctic and raise the new generation they'll bring to meet us next spring.

Now the snow and ice have all melted; warm breezes flowing over the land awaken the purple and yellow crocuses along the front pathway. Daffodils open in bright bursts of sunny yellow, while the tulips poke up their fat, green buds. The trees in the gully quiver with hundreds of returning birds, filling the air with their early morning songs that bring up the sun each day. The nesting begins.

Easter weekend is just over. This year we spent it in Toronto, meeting the family at one of the many beautiful hotels that tower above the inner-city pavement. After the cold winter, it was ecstasy to lounge around the warm pool, eat exquisitely prepared food in the beautiful restaurant decorated in an Oriental motif, and attend the musical adaptation of Victor Hugo's renowned classic, *Les Miserables*. It seemed appropriate to view this play on Easter weekend because of the chord of unbroken goodness that sings its way through a plot filled with injustice and sadness, a chord that can never be completely severed despite all the evil in mankind's heart.

Easter Sunday, we walked the few blocks to a large, old church in the heart of the city. When it was built over a hundred years ago, its spire soared above all the other buildings. Now, it is dwarfed alongside the glass sky scrapers that curve around it almost touching its ancient bricks. Yet, it remains, still dispensing Christ's lovely story of hope to all who will listen, and on Easter Sunday, at least, it was filled with people coming to be blessed by the triumphant message of the cross.

My favourite stone I now hold in my hand — dark slate-gray and heavy, it fits smoothly in my palm. A line of deep coral granite, about one quarter of an inch wide, encircles one end of the stone, and miraculously, within that elongated rose circle, there is a slim green cross. How thrilled I was when I picked it up from the beach one day, and since then I often study it trying to fathom the depths of what the cross means.

For us Protestants, the empty or plain cross speaks of resurrection and new life, while the crucifix one sees in Catholic churches and institutions, with Christ still hanging on it, portrays suffering and sacrifice. The message of Easter is that we can't have one without the other — resurrection and eternal life come out of Jesus' suffering and death. Although I'd been a Christian all my life, it was years before I began to understand the message of the cross — a message I'm still deciphering.

Jesus' painful death, with blood dripping from his nail-torn hands and feet, shocked and bewildered me. Why did it have to be this way? What sense did it make? How did all that suffering and blood bring about *my* salvation and the forgiveness of *my* sins? St. Paul says in one of his letters that Jesus' crucifixion was an offense to the Jews and foolishness to the Greeks. For a long time, I sat very close to those Jews and Greeks. I believed the message because I knew I should, but I didn't really comprehend it, despite the fact I must have heard dozens of Easter sermons over the years.

In any event, one day, as I began to read the Old Testament book of Leviticus, the penny finally dropped, as the English say. At the very beginning of the book, Moses lays out God's plan for the forgiveness of sins, because He knew that to allow sin to pile up, never to be forgiven, would cause separation from Himself and lead to disaster.

Therefore, a man (or woman, I presume) chose the finest and costliest animal in his flock, one that would win all the ribbons at the Royal Winter Fair, and be of more value than the others, to present to God. Then, standing before the priests, the man laid his hands on the forehead of the animal, symbolically transferring all his sins and guilt to the young bull. When it was sacrificed and burned, the sins of the man died with the animal. The priests sprinkled the blood on the altar to indicate God's participation.

As I read those first few verses of Leviticus, what happened at the crucifixion dawned on me. Christ was the sacrificial animal (lamb) who took on all mankind's sins, obliterating them by his death on the cross. That's what all those Easter sermons, which I failed to completely understand, came down to. And because of Christ's death and spilled blood, all the grisly business of killing and sacrificing animals was done with — forever!

Not that God ever told Man to put all his trust in the ceremonial sacrificing of animals. Ceremony and ritual certainly have a place in the obedience and worship of God, but they can never take the place of a merciful heart. Old Testament prophets lashed out at the mechanical observances of burnt sacrifices, at fasting, and trite hymn singing, calling instead for God's people to feed the hungry, help the oppressed, and let "justice run down like water, and righteousness flow as a stream." (Amos 5:24)

Old Testament readings still speak volumes to us in this ostentatious age where power and wealth are not usually used to bring about justice and mercy. Our gin and tonic lifestyle — with drinks around the pool while the smoke from our barbecue wafts heavenward, with never a thought in our heads of all the children around the world dying from hunger and disease, is obscene. We may wear our gold crosses around our necks and dangle them from our ear lobes, but if our hearts are filled with greed and self-centredness, we dishonour God as much as the Old Testament people about whom the prophets railed.

The cross is the symbol of the Christian Church. It tops every Catholic church and adorns most Protestant communion tables. But when non-Christians observe our crosses what does it mean to *them*? Does it tell them that here they will find love, acceptance, and forgiveness? Will it say that those of us who follow the sign of the cross are a hopeful, peaceful, joyful people? If that were the message they received I think they'd flock to join us; sadly, in the past quarter century, instead of people rushing to our churches, members left in droves.

The people of this sad world are hurting in a way they've probably never hurt before, and what they need most is a place of succour, a place to bind up their wounds, where they receive hope. One would think that the church would be the obvious place to find this, but the fact of the matter is, we sit so stiffly in our long pews, facing each other's backs, that we often fail to notice that the person next to us is bleeding.

For a long time, whenever I remembered that desolate day when Robert's marriage was breaking up and I sat in a cold, strange church longing for support, bitterness rose in my throat. I thought the church had failed me in an hour of need. But what did I expect — that someone could read my troubled mind or see my hidden, breaking heart? That someone would recognize me as a stranger and not only welcome me, but sit down and talk to me? Why should I expect any of this? After all, the ministers were probably worn out from counselling people all week, and the members probably had enough sorrows of their own, and more demands on their time and emotional strength than they could bear already. So why should I expect to find solace, understanding, and support in the church? I expected it because the Bible teaches us that the body of Christ (the church) is a place of caring and healing. "Come to me, all you who are heavy laden," said Jesus. And again, "Let people see you are my followers by the way you love one another."

Ever since that day I can't go into any church without looking around and wondering who of my fellow Christians is sitting nearby with a full or breaking heart. Because of the brave masks we wear, no one can tell.

There must be a way of getting in touch with the hurting ones right when they need it most. Filling out those printed forms in the hymnbook rack is of little use to someone who needs the loving touch of another human at that very moment. Surely every congregation has caring, sensitive members who could form a Caring Committee to act on the spot.

Just recently I heard of a congregation where this is done — a notice in the bulletin advises anyone in dire need to go to a certain room in the church where they will be met by someone who will hear them out and direct their needs to someone who can be of assistance — whether it be just a listening ear, or some other practical form of help. Maybe only two or three people call on that Caring Committee in the course of a year, but surely it fills an important Christian role. Jesus warned that when we fail to feed the hungry, visit the sick, *or* help the lonely stranger (who may have been sitting next to us in church for years), we do so at our peril.

Coffee times after the service are great for bonding members who habitually meet and visit, but are of little help to the stranger looking for some kindly fellowship. I've stood awkwardly holding my cup of coffee among dozens of members chatting amicably together, and felt more alone than if I were in a room by myself. If the coffee time is to be of any use to a newcomer, there must be hosts stationed around to seek them out.

On only one occasion did Art and I experience a warm welcome, in all our years of visiting churches; the moment we walked in the door, two gentlemen detached themselves from a group in the hall to greet us. After the service, they were at our elbows again, inviting us to the coffee room where they introduced us around, but never leaving us on our own. That church will always have a warm spot in our hearts. Lay people can't blame their minister if their church is unfriendly, they are the ones upon whom that reputation is built.

Newcomers should not be expected to be the ones to push back the cool exteriors to find a warm spot for themselves in the church, yet, so often, that is the case. It's true few people have the self confidence to approach strangers to welcome them and show them around. It might be a good idea to conduct short seminars in the social skills required.

Many churches decry the fact that their membership is declining and that few new people are joining. But wherever one is fortunate enough to find a friendly, welcoming congregation, one usually observes the membership growing — because the body of Christ is performing one of its main functions.

Sometimes the church lets people down because of its fear of disturbing the status quo, panicking when the unfamiliar arises. Over twenty years ago when I was superintendent of the Sunday School, we had an eighteen-year-old young man group-teaching a class of young children. I had known John since he was a tiny wisp of a baby whom his parents adored. A delicate child, he was small for his age, but he owned a sweet singing voice and loved to perform in church and Sunday School. Somewhat awkward, and not adept at sports, he liked to dress up in old clothes and play house with the little girls. As he was the same age as one of our children, he often played at our house or came for lunch once they started school.

He grew to be a sensitive young fellow, but somewhat of a misfit — not wanting to rough-house with the boys.

One time, we had tickets to the Ice Follies in London and suddenly had an extra ticket because one of our children couldn't go. I racked my mind trying to think of someone to ask at the last minute. Then, remembering how John loved dramatics and colour, I called him. "Oh, Mrs. Whilsmith," he cried, "you just answered my prayer!"

John grew up, loved small children, and offered to teach at Sunday School. All went well, until one morning I received a chilling call from one of the mothers saying she wasn't sending her little girl to Sunday School because she had just learned John was a homosexual. She, like many others in those days, felt

homosexuality and paedophilia went hand in hand. She told me
other mothers were not sending their children to Sunday School
either as long as John continued to teach.

I was stunned. Leaving for the church early, I awaited the
arrival of the young woman who shared the teaching duties with
John. Taking her aside, I asked her frankly if she had ever seen
him act in any inappropriate way with the children. "Never!"
she replied. Then she informed me that she and John planned to
take the children on a picnic in the park that very afternoon. It
was bad timing, and although I was positive the children were
in no danger, I admonished her, nevertheless, "Don't let him or
any of the children out of your sight." She promised.

My heart was heavy. I knew it was possible John was a
homosexual, but I couldn't believe this gentle young man was
a menace to anyone. His mother was a friend and a faithful
church worker. What effect would this have on her?

The next day, the minister sought me out at work. He, too,
had had several calls from irate parents. "I'm afraid we'll have
to ask John to stop teaching the class," he said.

I couldn't agree, not only because I was sure he wouldn't
hurt anyone, but because it would devastate his mother. "I know
you're my minister and I am only one in your congregation," I
told my minister, "but I also know that long after you've moved
from this congregation, John's mother will still be part of it,
sitting with me in the same pew. If you insist on John leaving,
I'll never be able to look her in the eye again, so if John goes I
must leave the church too!" It was a soul wrenching moment for
both of us.

In the end, John stayed on for two more weeks, and left of
his own accord, having got wind, I'm sure, of the ruckus.
Rumour had it he was in the city performing as a male stripper.
Would it have ended differently if we had accepted him just as
he was? I don't know.

Because the church is made up of imperfect 'living stones,'
it has faults and does make mistakes. There have been days
when I felt it forsook me. A few times I had to withdraw, to sit
alone with God to work out my problems and frustrations, but
even when I was most bereft, I was always overwhelmed with
such homesickness for the body of Christ I had to return. I found

out it wasn't so much a matter of me being a part of the church, as it was the church being a part of me. I wasn't whole without it.

When my friend Pat returned from wintering in Florida this year, she told me about walking into a strange church in another country and feeling so at home. "Isn't it marvellous," she mused, "how we can hear the same sweet story no matter where we go?" She's right.

Another friend, Elizabeth, and I celebrated our retirements by taking an around-the-world tour in 1984, and everywhere we went we found evidence of the Christian Church. Sometimes we had to search for it, but it *was* there. Above the masses thronging Tokyo's Ginza, a cross soars on the top of a tall building, a sign that Christianity shares space with Japanese commerce.

In Hong Kong, overcome with the crowds, the smells and squalor in the midst of great opulence, we slipped into a lovely Anglican church that was squashed in among other buildings, to soak up the peace and calm of a Lenten service. It was as if we'd come home. Even in China, which had just opened its borders to a few tourists at that time, we found a place where Christians met at great risk in a squalid part in the city.

Christianity has been in India since early times, and we encountered one man who proudly traced his Christian roots back to the sixth century. Christ's loving message of healing and hope is found wherever one travels, and it binds us together in a most wonderful way. The recent upsurge of Christianity in Russia and other former Eastern Block countries is evidence that it can never be stamped out regardless of the fervour and cruelty of its adversaries.

We know Christianity won't be stamped out in this country either, but it is distressing to live in an age when supporters are dwindling and when interest seems to be on the wane. It's sad to see many parents so casual about their children's religious education. Most believe they are enlightened when they say, "I don't want to force my children to go to Sunday School or church. When they grow up they can make that decision for themselves." These same loving parents wouldn't dream of leaving a loaded gun in their child's room with the attitude that when the child grows up he'll decide whether or not to pull the trigger. The parent knows the child will probably harm himself with the gun long before he reaches maturity. Growing up without religious beliefs is just as dangerous.

Children are like little dry sponges soaking up everything around them, be it good or bad. They love the Bible stories and, if given a chance, understand them better than many adults. Our little granddaughter Danielle comes to visit often and loves to hear stories from the big Bible book, and to learn the hymns I sang as a child. One night, as she cuddled down to go to sleep, she sighed, "Oh, I do love Jesus but I *wish* he'd come to our house!" Fortunately, Easter was near so we talked about Jesus' spirit being alive and always with us. Children who never learn about this kind of comfort and strength are greatly deprived, in my opinion, because they, too, have fears and troubles and they need to know they can look to a loving God for help.

Much of what is wrong in our society stems from the fact that children are not taught the difference between good and evil, right and wrong. Not that I'm suggesting this can only be done in a Christian home. Of course not. But despite its many failings, and where Jesus' words have not been distorted and corrupted by mankind's disobedience and arrogance, Christianity's history has been one of mercy and justice. Children should know that throughout the ages, dedicated followers of Christ were inspired to change laws, improve education, and provide hospitals. Furthermore, the very foundation of democracy came out of the Judaic/Christian religions.

It's a blot against Christianity that so few of us are involved in improving the social ills of our own day, and that we think so little about carrying on Christian traditions, many of which came down to us at a great cost to hundreds of lives. Still, there are always the faithful in each generation.

I hold in my hand this dark rock with its thin green cross embedded in it. Clean, smooth and beautiful it's not at all like the rough, bloody cross on which Christ was slain. Nevertheless, it reminds me that the cross is the cornerstone of Christianity, and I'm eternally grateful for all those souls who kept the faith alive to be passed on.

FOOTPRINTS IN THE SAND

Chapter X

Early this morning I walked down to the lake. It had rained in the night, washing the beach clean. It had been two or three weeks since I found any interesting stones, but today beautiful stones kept popping out at me. I picked up several ring-of-love stones — one was jet black with a bright pink band, speaking to me again of God's all-encircling love. Two splendid fossils also appeared at my feet — a perfectly preserved prehistoric creature with the dimensions and shape of an earwig, and another rock that looked for all the world like a piece of honeycomb with all its five-sided cells. I turned the fossils over in my hand recalling once more God's act of creation that began eons ago.

And I could hardly believe my eyes when I bent to pick up a chalk-white stone with a round hole through it; despite all my searching it was only the second one I'd found in fourteen years! Was God sending me another sign? Perhaps He was just affirming He still guides me along.

A clear set of footprints in the wet sand told me someone else had walked on the beach before me this morning. How many footsteps, I wonder, have been traced on this beach going back to the Native Canadians who built their fires here, and the early explorers who traversed the expansive rim of Lake Huron? Footprints of others lead us all on, but unlike the prints in the sand which the waves soon wash away, the footprints of our ancestors remain forever.

Travelling across this great country I am always awe-struck by the mammoth task faced by our pioneers to clear the

land, push roads and railways lines through dense bush, grow
the first crops, open the first schools, churches, and hospitals.
Because they worked unrelentingly to building a nation, we,
their descendants, live in a country second to none.

Because my great-grandparents settled in Canada, rather
than the United States of America, I am a Canadian, and it's
mainly due to the fact that my own parents decided to live and
work in a certain area that I am where I am and what I am today.
My life is immeasurably blessed because I follow in their
footsteps.

In the dim, distant past, farther back than we can trace, an
ancestor decided to devote his/her life to God and become a
Christian. That decision affected all succeeding generations.
Years ago, when JoAnne, as a teenager, disagreed with the
limits placed on her by her father and me, the worst insult she
could hurl at us was *"Puritans!"*

"You're right," we'd answer, "but remember, that same
Puritan blood is flowing through your veins, too, whether you
like it or not!" The footprints are there.

Anita's children, Heather and Duncan, began coming to us
for holidays when they were little more than babies, and loved
the beach, skipping through the water, the waves splashing their
faces, the wind ruffling their hair.

One day as we ran on the shore, I looked behind to see
Heather, her small pink legs stretched out to keep up with me.
"Look, Grandma," she called above the wind, "I'm going in
your footsteps." She leapt along planting her tiny feet in the
prints I left in the wet sand. Later that night when I remembered
her remark, I wondered if I'd want her to "go" in my steps.
Certainly not all, I decided, but perhaps my footsteps may act
as a warning, as well as a guide.

Heather is now twenty-one, her long, brown legs far out-
strip mine on the beach these days. I'm the one running to keep
up. Already she's gleaned more knowledge than I have in my
whole lifetime, and is about to graduate from university, ready
to face the high-tech world in which she'll live and work. Life
will be much different for her than it was for me, with limitless
opportunities and expanding freedoms. But in all this, she, too,
will have to choose between right and wrong, good and evil. I

pray truth, integrity, kindness, mercy, and honour will be as important to her and all our grandchildren, as they were to many of their ancestors — that they will face bravely the disappointments and changes that will surely come in their lives.

Changes come to all of us. Thank God for that. Who of us would want to remain a baby forever, no matter how comfortable and coddled we were? And who could continue perpetually in the confusing, confounding world of a teenager, or endure forever those middle years of battling for recognition and success while raising a family. Surely it would be more than any human soul could stand. It is *good* to move on.

Henry Van Dyke wrote that moving day goes on all the days of our lives — "from house to house we move, from youth to age — from opinion to opinion." It's amazing how our opinions do shift — things I was sure of just a few years ago, I no longer believe. And that's not frivolity, it's wisdom! Some changes, however, are not to our liking.

When Duncan was four he came for holidays all by himself for the first time. How proud he was, dragging in his heavy suitcase, a wide grin lighting up his small face. All went well except for mealtimes when, pushing away his plate, he constantly scowled, "Mommy doesn't make it like that," or "Mommy doesn't make me eat this stuff," or "I hate this junk."

After three days I'd had more than enough. Sitting him down I spoke sternly, "Listen to me, Duncan, we go on holidays for a change, and eating different kinds of food is part of it. If you didn't want a change, perhaps you should have stayed at home!" Fixing me with his unblinking blue eyes, blond hair straight up on end, he growled, "Grandma, I came here to change my people, not my food!"

Like Duncan, many of us only accept the changes we enjoy, not the ones that upset our lives or make demands on us. However, Van Dyke is right, life is constantly changing whether we want it to or not, and moving from "youth to age" is not only challenging and disconcerting, it is sometimes downright depressing.

There's a paradox in growing older — part of us remains forever the lovely, innocent child, the searching teenager, the confident twenty-two-year-old, but although we remain all of

what we were before, we still move on to become different
people. Some will mature into better, kinder, sweeter elders;
others will become bitter, pessimistic, and angry.

Several years ago, I worked as an interviewer for the
Psychology Department of a nearby university that was conducting a study on *Life Satisfaction of Seniors Living in Rural
Ontario.* Over a period of two years I talked to many elderly
citizens, all picked at random; some I saw only once or twice,
others I visited several times.

In the beginning, I asked specific questions and filled out
forms, but later I delved more deeply into the participants' lives.
Most of them were in their seventies and eighties, and as I
listened to them, definite patterns formed. All had come through
hard times — wars, depressions, the death of loved ones, serious illnesses, and accidents. A few raged at what life had dealt
them; some were resigned but sad, while others remained cheerful and brimming with hope. One might assume that those who
suffered the most would be the most pessimistic, and those who
had had the least hardship would turn out to be the most
cheerful, but that wasn't the case.

Two women I remember especially. One lady's life was a
bleak story of parents dying when she was an infant, of being
adopted but losing those parents too, of an illness that hospitalized her for years, of a husband who deserted her, and of
children who failed. Yet, she didn't know the meaning of
self-pity, and in the home-for-the-aged where she lived she
constantly spread cheer and hope to others. We became friends,
and I continued to visit her long after the study was finished.
One day, years later, I found her very ill and near death. She
opened her eyes and whispered, "Oh Gwyn, I've just been
thinking what an 'interesting' life I've had!" To the very end
she remained cheerful.

The other lady's life was also tragic. Two of her young
children died in an epidemic, and her husband was killed in an
accident while in his prime. The story of her struggle to keep
the rest of the family together through terrible hardships brought
tears to my eyes. Yet she, too, continued to look on the bright
side of life.

"What's your secret?" I asked. After a thoughtful moment, she replied, "I think it's being able to accept the changes whether they be good or bad because change will come, and if you rail against it or fight it you'll likely become bitter, but if you flow with it, you'll find life is still worth the living." Her words stay with me to this day.

However, it's still a shock to pass a mirror and see this aging woman looking back at me, especially on a day when I'm feeling particularly fit. It seems a cruel joke that nature keeps us young inside while the outer body withers and weakens. My friend Shirley says, "It's not fair we should look old and still feel young — maybe it would be better if we grew old on the inside too!" I don't think so. The part of us that stays young is that which will last forever and will, someday, leave this failing physical body far behind. It's terribly important to keep that lasting part of us, which is our *real* selves, in good spirits. I'm thankful to have what my friend Pat calls "a happy heart." Of course, I suffer disappointment or sadness and even depression, but I can never retain those moods long; my soul wearies of them and has to be happy again.

Aunty Mar, aged eighty-six, thinks it's a pity we have to deal with all the hard things (arthritis, heart problems, hearing loss, low energy) when we're old and weak. She believes we could handle these trials better when we're young, but I'm not so sure. The young never anticipate problems and troubles, and are so intense that they view every setback or disappointment as a lasting catastrophe. If we elders haven't learned anything else surely we know that every sorrow or hardship eventually passes over, and life goes on.

Old age, however, does not pass over. When we're twenty, five years is a long time, one quarter of our whole life, and the years stretch out ahead. When we're over seventy, we know we may not even be here in another five years. It does change one's perspective, and perhaps it's the reason elders find the days, weeks, and years flying by. It's quite normal, I think, when people come to their later years to have times of panic — feeling there's still so much to do and so little time left. It's not surprising some of them become depressed, especially when one also considers the real possibility of failing health. Very few people I know fear death — what they are afraid of is dementia or a long debilitating illness.

Still, one has to believe that God remains with us even if that happens. One day when I was browsing through the book of Isaiah, my heart was lifted by these words:

> I have cared for you from the time you were born.
> I am your God and will take care of you until you are old and your hair is grey.
> I made you and will care for you.
> I will give you help and rescue you.

Art and I watched our parents die — his father instantaneously from a heart attack; my mother after ten years of heart disease; his mother and my father after they had both suffered long and painfully, especially Art's mother who had cancer of the mouth. It was a torturous experience for them and their loved ones, but there was never a time when we believed we weren't supported and covered with God's love.

How unbearable it would have been for us, however, to believe the lives of these once strong, vibrant people ended with their earthly deaths.

What it all comes down to, in the end, is trusting God, not only with our lives, but with our deaths too. Aunty Mar trusts Him, believes all her loved ones — her parents, brothers, sister, and husband — are all just waiting for her to cross the line. I think she already lives with one foot in heaven, always conversing with God and her dear departed. Her blue eyes shine, "I can hardly wait to see them all again. Won't we have a celebration?" Yes, sometime in the future there will be a party for Aunty Mar, but in the meantime, she plants her garden every spring, plans a trip to Portugal next winter, and hopes her little dog will have another litter of pups. She may live with one foot in heaven, but she still has one firmly planted in this world which she still loves so well. Surely that is what all of us desire — not to be afraid to face death, whether it comes soon or late, while still enjoying all the blessings of this earth, knowing we are always in God's hands.

How does one learn to trust God? Much the same way we learn to trust a human friend who doesn't desert us in difficult

times, even when we make grievous mistakes, and who cele-
brates our joys and small triumphs as if they were her/his own.
Who is always there for us.

Because my mentor-friend Pat understands me so well, I
trust her with my deepest questions and doubts, sure she will
never be shocked or turn her back on me. How much more
should I be able to trust the God who created me, has known me
since before my birth, blesses me beyond all reason, and loves
me so intimately that He even knows the number of hairs on my
head!

A woman in deep trouble sat across the kitchen table,
pouring out her woes to a Christian friend. "How I wish I had a
faith like yours," she cried. "Please give me some."

Although faith in God can't be passed out like chocolate
chip cookies, it can be attained by everyone. "Taste and see that
the Lord is good," sings the psalmist. We must 'taste,' or try and
experience God's faithfulness to know He is worthy of our trust.
Faith in God is never passive; it moves, changes and deepens.
I've attended Christian churches where nothing but 'salvation'
is preached over and over, with no maturing or moving on. Paul
knew when people first became followers of Christ, they were
like babies needing their bottle of milk every few hours. But
milk bottles are for infants, and he urged his hearers to grow up
in the faith until they could eat and digest 'meat.'

Our littlest grandson Owen had his bottle long after it
should have been thrown out, but because he was often sick, his
parents allowed him to take it to bed for comfort. One day he
bit the end off the nipple. "That's it, Owen," his mother told
him, "that's the end of the nipples, so no more bottles."

"Oh, mommy," he sobbed, "it's so, so sad." The day after,
he bragged he was now such a big boy he didn't need a bottle,
and in a few days his appetite for good, solid food improved
dramatically.

Unfortunately, many of us Christians still hold on to our
precious milk bottles and the soppy faith that goes with them.
Of course, we believe Christ is the Saviour and Lord of our lives,
but having accepted that wonderful gift, it behooves us to move
on, to free ourselves from the narrow religious-legalism that
Jesus discounted, and venture out to do something for God —

to make our lives count for Him. I don't think God is going to judge me by the number of times I went to church, or how fluent I was in quoting scripture, or even the number of hours I spent in prayer, important as all that is. God will, however, be very interested in the amount of love I showed to my fellow beings, how many I helped or turned away in their time of need.

Jesus surprised his listeners when He raised the question of who would be accepted into the Kingdom of God. He told that parable which declared that those recognized by God will be the ones who feed the hungry, clothe the naked, and visit the prisoners. Those who go around crying "Lord, Lord," all the time will not necessarily be accepted by God, he said. Faith without works is a dead thing, declares the writer of the book of James.

Time and again, the Bible exhorts us to love one another, going so far as to state if we don't love one another, we really do not love God either. Jesus' final commandment was to love as He had loved; the world should be able to recognize His followers by the love they showed to others. He didn't mean sitting around gushing over each other — His kind of love is full of action and much tougher. It's also often risky and painful. Every time you open yourself to love someone, you set yourself up for disappointment and hurt. Recently, our young minister, quoting Buddha, pointed out, "He who loves fifty has fifty woes; he who loves ten has ten woes; he who loves none has no woes." The deeper your love, the deeper may be your hurt.

Some Christians find it difficult to even love other Christians and can't agree on how we should approach God, or how He should come to us. It's such a useless exercise since God comes to each of us in His own special, intimate way. George MacDonald wrote a lovely piece about God coming to us down his own secret stair. This God, who understands us so completely, far better than anyone else, including ourselves, knows everything about us — the parents we've had, the genes and personalities we're born with, our deep struggles — and knowing all this, comes to us down His own secret stair.

How can I ever presume to know how anyone else should come to God, or have the audacity to insist that everyone experience God as I do? To do so is to put limits on Him who is all powerful and knowing, and to deny His grace and mercy. Because I experience His grace and mercy every day, I trust Him with His judgment which I will face one day. Thank God I will not be judged by my peers, or even my friends whom I may have hurt or disappointed. Their verdict might be very harsh, but God, who understands everything about me, will judge me with mercy. I love Pat's story of the Jehovah Witnesses who came to her door one day trying to frighten her into the Kingdom by insisting there were not many places left. Pat, so gentle and kind, and never comfortable rebuking anyone, replied, "Well, I'm sure I'll see you up there!"

C.S. Lewis's *The Great Divorce* is a powerful allegory of heaven, where we may, indeed, be surprised about whom we meet there — maybe our worst enemies! Another favourite writer Madeleine L'Engle says some people won't be happy in heaven unless they can see their enemies burning in hell. How disappointing it will be if their enemies don't get their just desserts!

I prefer to leave all that up to God who created us all and who sent His Son Jesus to explain and live out His great love, a love so tender and sweet Jesus said we could even call God Daddy (or, I'm sure Mommy, if we want to). When I was small I called my father Papa. I loved him and trusted him with my life. My heavenly Papa I love even more dearly and I trust Him with my life and death and whatever comes after.

What comfort we derive from those lovely words of Jesus:

> There are many rooms in my Father's house, and I am going to prepare a place for you. If this were not so I would not tell you . . . I will come back and take you to myself so that you will be where I am.

What more could we ask for?

A few days after my mother died, we found a portion of a poem by Robert Louis Stevenson pasted on the fly leaf of her Bible. It brought great comfort and hope to those she left behind:

> No funeral gloom, my dears when I am gone;
> Corpse-gazings, tears, black raiment, graveyard grimness.

Think of me as withdrawn into the dimness,
Yours still, you mine. Remember all the best
Of our past moments and forget the rest;
And so, to where I wait, come gently on.

Gently, gently I travel on, hoping to arrive not too soon, but not too late, either — carrying my basket of stones, leaving my footprints behind me.